A LITERARY GUIDE TO Flannery O'Connor's Georgia

A LITERARY GUIDE TO
Flannery O'Connor's Georgia

Sarah Gordon

with Craig Amason, Consulting Editor

Contemporary photographs by Marcelina Martin

THE UNIVERSITY OF GEORGIA PRESS   ATHENS

*Publication of this book was made possible in part by
a generous grant from the Watson-Brown Foundation, Inc.*

Designed by Erin Kirk New
Set in Adobe Garamond Pro
Printed and bound by Everbest Printing Company
for Four Colour Imports

The paper in this book meets the guidelines for
permanence and durability of the Committee on
Production Guidelines for Book Longevity of the
Council on Library Resources.

Printed in China

12 11 10 09 08 P 5 4 3 2 1

Library of Congress Cataloging-in-Publication Data

Gordon, Sarah, 1941–
A literary guide to Flannery O'Connor's Georgia /
Sarah Gordon with Craig Amason, consulting editor ;
contemporary photographs by Marcelina Martin.
p.   cm.
Includes bibliographical references and index.
ISBN-13: 978-0-8203-2763-1 (pbk. : alk. paper)
ISBN-10: 0-8203-2763-8 (pbk. : alk. paper)
    1. O'Connor, Flannery—Homes and haunts—
Georgia. 2. Authors, American—Homes and
haunts—Georgia. 3. Georgia—In literature. 4. Literary
landmarks—Georgia. I. Amason, Craig. II. Martin,
Marcelina, 1950– III. Title.
PS3565.C57Z6798   2008
813'.54—dc22   2007038320

Maps by Deborah Reade

TO THE MEMORY OF Robert W. Mann AND Margaret Florencourt Mann

CONTENTS

ACKNOWLEDGMENTS

WE ARE GRATEFUL to the late Hugh Brown, for his early dedication to honoring the achievement of Flannery O'Connor; Gillian Brown and Rena Patton of the Flannery O'Connor Childhood Home in Savannah; Pat Persse of Savannah; Nancy Davis Bray of Special Collections in the Ina Dillard Russell Library, Georgia College & State University; Mary Jo Thompson of the former Sanford House Restaurant, Milledgeville; Matt Davis and Jim Turner of the Old Governor's Mansion, Milledgeville; the late Robert W. Mann for the donation of photographs; Joe McTyre for the 1962 photographs of O'Connor; Brother Callistus of the Monastery of the Holy Spirit, Conyers; the Reverend Michael McWhorter of Sacred Heart Catholic Church, Milledgeville; Monsignor William O'Neill, Rector of the Cathedral of St. John the Baptist; and the Watson-Brown Foundation.

The authors are grateful to the *New Georgia Encyclopedia* (www.georgia encyclopedia.org) for providing much of the historical information in this guide.

Mary Flannery O'Connor, age three, reading intently. Courtesy, Flannery O'Connor Collection, Georgia College & State University Library

INTRODUCTION: Who Is Flannery O'Connor?

FLANNERY O'CONNOR (1925–64) is one of the great American story-tellers, a woman whose brief life was dedicated to the pursuit of her art. O'Connor's stories and novels have as their bedrock a profound Christianity, for Flannery O'Connor was a devout Roman Catholic. Unlike most of her postwar contemporaries—Saul Bellow, Bernard Malamud, Eudora Welty, and John Updike, for example—O'Connor always concerned herself in her fiction with spiritual matters. The here-and-now serves her as an avenue to asking the most compelling questions of our existence, those involving the meaning and purpose of life as viewed under the aspect of eternity.

O'Connor's work is strongly indebted to her sense of place; the South becomes a microcosm of the macrocosm, wherein the battle between good and evil, sin and redemption, is played out. Although O'Connor witnessed the memorable inception of the civil rights movement, she repeatedly presents racism as a failure of the charity that Christ embodied. O'Connor was not, however, a writer with a political or social agenda. Neither mythic stories of the so-called Old South nor the increasing urbanization (and suburbanization) of America and the South merited a central place in her fiction. Instead, she repeatedly attacks smugness, superiority, and, most importantly, unbelief. In Flannery O'Connor's world, all of us are displaced people, imbued with the capacity for willfulness and arrogance because of original sin. Our foolish trust in progress and technology leads us to a false sense of autonomy, to selfishness, and to manipulation of others. Above

"If you're a writer and the South is what you know, then it's what you'll write about and how you judge it will depend on how you judge yourself. It's perhaps good and necessary to get away from it physically for a while, but this is by no means to escape it. I stayed away from the time I was 20 until I was 25 with the notion that the life of my writing depended on my staying away. I would certainly have persisted in that delusion had I not got very ill and had to come home. The best of my writing has been done here." (*The Habit of Being*)

all, we forget our creatureliness and the concomitant need for humility. In her first published book, *Wise Blood* (1952), O'Connor boldly captures the modernist attempt to deny the Fall and the existence of sin and therefore the need for redemption. As Hazel Motes attempts to establish his Church Without Christ, he does not realize that, on the streets of the modern secular city, he is preaching to the converted. To Haze's credit, however, he can never free himself of the "stinking mad shadow of Jesus moving from tree to tree in the back of his mind." Try as he might, Haze cannot, finally, deny sin and his need for atonement.

O'Connor's obedience to the Church never precluded her questioning and exploration of its dogma, for as a follower of St. Thomas Aquinas, she firmly believed that one should use one's reason in matters of faith, though reason is, of course, limited. As an intellectual Catholic (who would never have tolerated being described in such a way), O'Connor read deeply in theology and philosophy and often chastised her fellow Catholics for their superficial reading habits and desire for easy "inspiration." Her fiction makes it clear that belief is not easy, for, as she wrote, "What people don't realize is how much religion costs. They think faith is a big electric blanket, when of course it is the cross."

Readers of O'Connor's letters, most of which are collected and edited in the prize-winning collection *The Habit of Being* (1979), are aware of the author's candor and conviction in spiritual matters. Here is no evidence of the saccharine "Pious Style," which O'Connor abhorred; instead O'Connor's vast theological reading and understanding are everywhere evident. Deeply versed in Thomistic thought, O'Connor read the twentieth-century Catholic apologists as well: Jacques Maritain, Etienne Gilson, Gabriel Marcel, Romano Guardini, and even the (then) somewhat controversial Teilhard de Chardin. In 2007 Emory University opened the full correspondence of Flannery O'Connor to Betty Hester, the correspondent named simply "A" in *The Habit of Being*. Many of these letters had not been published in the collected letters, and readers will there discover additional insights into

Flannery O'Connor at the autograph party for Wise Blood *on the GCSU campus in 1952. Courtesy, Flannery O'Connor Collection, GCSU Library*

O'Connor's life. One of O'Connor's close friends and an aspiring writer, an avid reader, and a struggling Catholic, Hester clearly valued her exchanges on literature and spirituality with O'Connor. Readers of all of O'Connor's letters may see a fine Christian apologist, sophisticated in her reading and understanding, but possessed of a strong personal faith that was surely tested by illness and pain.

Her tough-mindedness extended to her subject matter and style as well. In fact, some family members recall that her cousin Katie Semmes was so appalled when she read *Wise Blood* that she went to bed for a week. Other relatives were equally shocked, admittedly curious about just exactly how Flannery knew anything about prostitutes or blaspheming street preachers. Of course, such tactics were intentional on the writer's part, for O'Connor believed that contemporary readers needed to be shocked out of their indifference or complacency to consider life's greatest concern: their salvation. "For the hard of hearing you shout," she wrote, "and for the almost blind you draw large and startling figures."

Perhaps it is presumptuous to link the vivid images of O'Connor's fertile imagination to specific scenes within the author's actual sight, but no visitor to Georgia who knows the work of O'Connor can miss the red clay roads, the long tree-lined vistas, and the quirky ambience of rural and small-town life that provide the settings for much of her work. To assert that Georgia "places" were a catalyst to her writing in no way denies O'Connor's genius its depth and flair; it is merely to demonstrate that her intense knowledge of place and the familiar served her well. She herself once said that even if her stories were set in Japan, her characters would still talk like Georgia politician Eugene Talmadge.

Although O'Connor's narratives leave the realm of the everyday as they gather momentum, O'Connor depends on her knowledge of the rural South for the "accidents" of her work; its essence or substance is, of course, universal. O'Connor's "view of the woods" enables her to people her fiction with characters and scenes that are—even in their exaggeration and strangeness—recognizably southern, though they are certainly, and above all, broadly human and profoundly familiar.

CHRONOLOGY

1925 Mary Flannery O'Connor is born on March 25, the only child of Edward Francis O'Connor and Regina Cline O'Connor. The O'Connors live at 207 E. Charlton Street in Savannah on Lafayette Square, just across from the Cathedral of St. John the Baptist.

1931 Mary Flannery enters the first grade at St. Vincent's Grammar School for Girls in Savannah.

1936 Mary Flannery transfers to Sacred Heart Grammar School in Savannah.

1938 Edward O'Connor becomes a zone real estate appraiser for the Federal Housing Administration and the family moves to Atlanta, living at 2525 Potomac Street. Mary Flannery attends North Fulton High School.

1940 Because of Edward O'Connor's failing health from systemic lupus erythematosus, the family moves to Milledgeville into the Cline family home located at 311 W. Greene Street, where they live with Mary Flannery's aunts, Mary and Katie Cline. Mary Flannery enrolls in Peabody High School on the campus of Georgia State College for Women (GSCW).

1941   Edward O'Connor dies on February 1 from complications of lupus.

1942   Mary Flannery graduates from Peabody High School and enrolls in summer classes at GSCW.

1945   Mary Flannery receives her BA degree in social science from GSCW in June and leaves to attend the State University of Iowa, where she receives a scholarship in journalism. Unhappy in this program, she enrolls in the Writers' Workshop, directed by Paul Engle. She now calls herself simply Flannery.

1947   Flannery receives her Master of Fine Arts degree from Iowa on June 1 and begins working on her first novel. She remains at Iowa on a Rinehart fellowship until June of 1948.

1948   Flannery receives an invitation to attend the Yaddo Foundation artists' retreat near Saratoga Springs, New York, where she stays through June and July and returns to reside from September through February 1949.

1949   Flannery lives in New York City through August and then moves to Ridgefield, Connecticut, to occupy a garage apartment at the home of Robert and Sally Fitzgerald. She continues to work diligently on her first novel, begun at Iowa.

1950   While traveling to Milledgeville for the Christmas holidays, Flannery becomes very ill and is hospitalized when she arrives.

1951   Flannery is transferred to Emory University Hospital in Atlanta in February, where blood tests confirm that she has lupus. By March she has recovered to the extent that she can return to Milledgeville. Flannery and Regina O'Connor move to the family farm, Andalusia, located four miles north of town.

1952	Flannery's first novel, *Wise Blood*, is published on May 15.
1955	Flannery's first collection of short stories, *A Good Man Is Hard to Find and Other Stories*, is published on June 6.
1958	At the end of April, Flannery and Regina O'Connor travel to Milan, Paris, Lourdes, and Rome. The pilgrimage is a gift from Mrs. Raphael Semmes ("Cousin Katie") of Savannah.
1960	Flannery's second novel, *The Violent Bear It Away*, is published on February 8.
1964	Flannery O'Connor dies in the Baldwin County (Milledgeville) Hospital shortly after midnight on August 3.
1965	Flannery's second collection of short stories, *Everything That Rises Must Converge*, is published.
1969	*Mystery and Manners: Occasional Prose,* edited by Sally and Robert Fitzgerald, is published.
1971	*Complete Stories* is published and wins the National Book Award for Fiction. The award has never before been given to the work of a dead writer.
1979	*The Habit of Being: Letters of Flannery O'Connor*, edited by Sally Fitzgerald, is published to much acclaim.
1988	*Flannery O'Connor: Collected Works,* edited by Sally Fitzgerald, is published in the distinguished Library of America series.

A LITERARY GUIDE TO Flannery O'Connor's Georgia

Mary Flannery's childhood home at 207 East Charlton Street

Savannah

MARY FLANNERY O'CONNOR was born at St. Joseph's Hospital in Savannah, Georgia, on March 25, 1925, into two of Georgia's oldest Catholic families, the Clines of middle Georgia and the O'Connors of Savannah. The Savannah of O'Connor's childhood was, of course, a decidedly smaller and more provincial version of the Savannah of today. Indeed, the hospital in which O'Connor was born is no longer standing. In the new St. Joseph's Hospital, a special wing is dedicated to the Flannery family, for whom Flannery O'Connor was named.

In fact, in the mid-1920s and early 1930s Savannah was no longer even the busy seaport and cotton capital it had become by the end of the nineteenth century; the damage done to the cotton crops by the boll weevil and changing economic patterns had significantly reduced the city's industry. The stock market crash of 1929 and the ensuing Great Depression hit Savannah and the young O'Connor family hard, though the Irish Catholic community of relatives and friends was extremely supportive of its own. The first thirteen years of O'Connor's life, spent in Savannah, were certainly crucial in the development of the mature writer. The city itself was a beautiful historic setting, and the majestic Cathedral of St. John the Baptist, located just across the square from O'Connor's childhood home at 207 E. Charlton Street, provided the bedrock of the young writer's faith.

St. Joseph's Hospital, the birthplace of Mary Flannery O'Connor. Courtesy of the Georgia Historical Society, Cordray-Foltz Collection

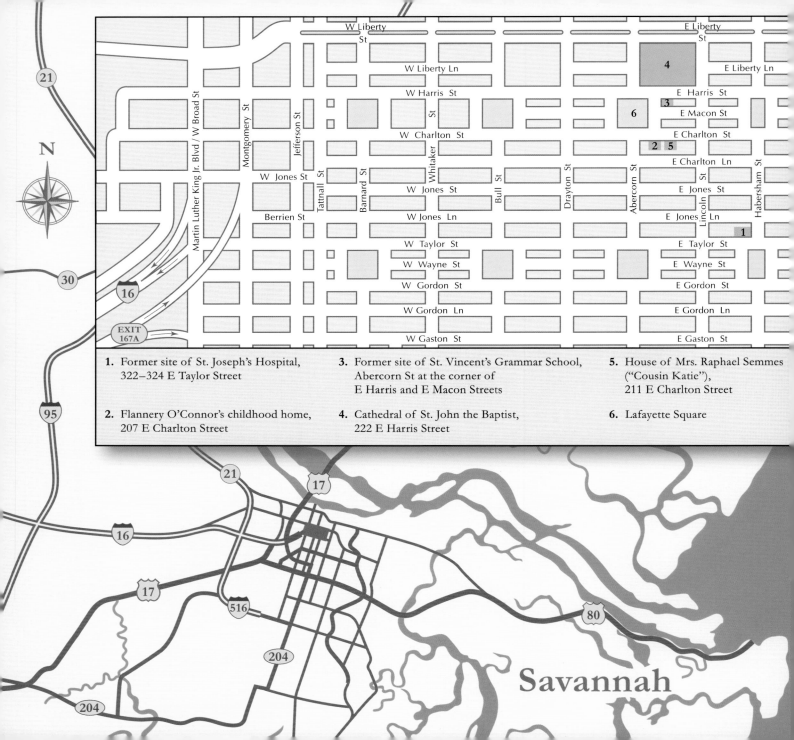

W Liberty St
E Liberty St
W Liberty Ln
E Liberty Ln
W Harris St
E Harris St
E Macon St
W Charlton St
E Charlton St
E Charlton Ln
W Jones St
E Jones St
W Jones Ln
E Jones Ln
Berrien St
W Taylor St
E Taylor St
W Wayne St
E Wayne St
W Gordon St
E Gordon St
W Gordon Ln
E Gordon Ln
W Gaston St
E Gaston St

Martin Luther King Jr. Blvd / W Broad St
Montgomery St
Jefferson St
Tattnall St
Barnard St
Whitaker St
Bull St
Drayton St
Abercorn St
Lincoln St
Habersham St

N

21
30
16
95
EXIT 167A

4
6
3
2 5
1

21
17
16
17
516
204
80
204

Savannah

1. Former site of St. Joseph's Hospital, 322–324 E Taylor Street

2. Flannery O'Connor's childhood home, 207 E Charlton Street

3. Former site of St. Vincent's Grammar School, Abercorn St at the corner of E Harris and E Macon Streets

4. Cathedral of St. John the Baptist, 222 E Harris Street

5. House of Mrs. Raphael Semmes ("Cousin Katie"), 211 E Charlton Street

6. Lafayette Square

The Flannerys and the O'Connors

Flannery O'Connor once joked, "I was brought up in Savannah where there was a colony of the Over-Irish. They have the biggest St. Patrick's Day parade anywhere around and generally go nutty on the subject." The Flannerys and the O'Connors were indeed distinguished members of that "Over-Irish" community.

A devout Roman Catholic, John Flannery immigrated to the United States from Ireland in 1851 at age sixteen and moved to Savannah in 1854, working as a clerk and bookkeeper. After enlisting in the Confederate Army, Flannery fought with Generals Johnston and Hood, though he had to leave the army before the 1865 surrender because of illness. When he returned to Savannah, he founded the Southern Bank of the State of Georgia, of which he was president. He was also an active railroad director and cotton broker and helped to build the Cathedral of St. John the Baptist in 1870. When that cathedral burned in 1898, he served on the building commission for the rebuilding of the church. He married Mary Ellen Norton, the granddaughter of Patrick Harty. John and Mary Ellen Flannery's daughter Kate married Raphael Semmes, a nephew of the Confederate admiral. She is Flannery's beloved "Cousin Katie," who lived next door to Ed and Regina O'Connor's home on E. Charlton Street and was very supportive of and generous to the young family. Mary Flannery O'Connor was named for the Flannery side of her patriarchal heritage, specifically for Mary Norton Flannery, mother of Kate Semmes, to honor Cousin Katie.

A strong-willed woman who drove one of the few electric cars in Savannah at the time, Cousin Katie actually held the deed for Ed O'Connor's house, and when the family left Savannah in 1938, Ed O'Connor, not having paid off the debt, relinquished the house to Mrs. Semmes. At her death in 1958, Mrs. Semmes willed the Charlton Street house to Flannery O'Connor, who renovated it and rented it out as apartments until the time of her death in 1964.

Monument to John Flannery in the Flannery family plot in the Catholic Cemetery, Savannah

Patrick O'Connor also immigrated to Savannah from Ireland in the late nineteenth century. Patrick, Flannery O'Connor's great-grandfather, was a wheelwright who eventually made wagons and carriages. His wheelwright shop was located on E. Broad Street in Savannah, between President and York streets. Patrick married Mary Cash, by whom he had ten children. One of his sons, Edward Francis, Flannery's grandfather, became a prominent banker and businessman in the city; his home at 115 W. Gwinnett Street still stands today. Edward O'Connor married Mary Elizabeth Golden in 1894; they had eight children. In an unusual double joining of the two families, Edward O'Connor's daughter Nan married Herbert Cline, brother of Regina Cline, and a short time later, in 1922, his son Edward Francis O'Connor Jr., known as Ed, married Regina, whom he had met at Herbert and Nan's wedding. They were wed in Sacred Heart Church in Milledgeville.

Ed O'Connor had attended Catholic schools in Savannah and graduated from Mount St. Mary's College in Emmitsburg, Maryland. In 1916 he entered the service in World War I, in which he served with distinction in France. After the war, he worked for his father, who ran a distributorship for candies and tobacco, until, financed by a gift from Katie Semmes in honor of the birth of Mary Flannery, he began a real estate business in Savannah, the Dixie Realty Company, which soon included the Dixie Construction Company. In 1933 he became president of Fulton Company Realtors. However, Ed O'Connor was more interested in his work with the American Legion than in selling real estate. He served as commander of Chatham Post 36 and chairman of the Veterans Council of Administration. Later, as Commander of the American Legion for the state of Georgia, he traveled a great deal and made speeches, which, his only child later recalled, made her proud of his patriotism.

Father and daughter were extremely close; Flannery acknowledged in a letter years later that her father had probably "toted" around in his pockets some of her early artistic productions: "I drew—mostly chickens, begin-

Mary Flannery's parents, Edward F. O'Connor and Regina Cline O'Connor. Courtesy, Flannery O'Connor Collection, GCSU Library

ning at the tail, the same chicken over and over. . . . Also occasional verse. My father wanted to write but had not the time or money or training or any of the opportunities I have had." She added, "I am never likely to romanticize him because I carry around most of his faults as well as his tastes. I even have about his same constitution: I have the same disease. . . . At the time he had it there was nothing for it but the undertaker. . . . Anyway, whatever I do in the way of writing makes me extra happy in the thought that it is a fulfillment of what he wanted to do himself."

In 1938 Ed O'Connor was made a real estate appraiser for the Federal Housing Authority, and, though he had not intended for his family to leave Savannah, the three moved to Atlanta for his new job.

The Flannery O'Connor Childhood Home

Located at 207 E. Charlton Street on Lafayette Square, Flannery O'Connor's childhood home is a traditional but unassuming Savannah row house. Purchased in 1989 by the newly established Flannery O'Connor Childhood Home Foundation through the efforts of Robert Burnett, president of Armstrong State College, and two Armstrong professors, Hugh Brown and Robert Strozier, the home is now open to visitors and serves as a gathering place for literary events.

A visit to this home provides valuable insight to readers and scholars of the work of Flannery O'Connor. The board of directors has filled the three-story home with furnishings of the 1925–38 period, including the large baby carriage used by Regina O'Connor for her daughter and the "kiddy koop" on the second floor in the parents' bedroom, a strange cradle that is screened on the sides and top to keep out insects, especially the mosquitoes of this humid climate. Mary Flannery's bedroom, next to that of her parents, is furnished with the actual twin beds and play table and chairs used by the O'Connors. In Flannery's childhood, the third floor (not yet accessible to

Home of Mrs. Raphael (Cousin Katie) Semmes on Charlton Street as it appears today

Pram used by the O'Connors for baby Mary Flannery

The "kiddie koop" cradle used for baby Mary Flannery

visitors) held, among other items, an unconnected claw-foot bathtub where little Mary Flannery and her friends liked to sit and read. One childhood friend recalls that Mary Flannery liked to be read to by a friend and often asked that a section of a book or story be repeated, much to the chagrin of the reader who would lose the flow of the narrative. Clearly, the young writer's imagination was already stirred by the power of story.

Friends recall that, during those years, Regina would invite several of Mary Flannery's friends over each week for the Saturday morning radio broadcast of *Let's Pretend* in the O'Connor living room, after which she would serve refreshments from the nearby kitchen. Surely this activity was fodder to young Mary Flannery's imagination, which grew to stretch its boundaries, though the child herself was well insulated and protected. Several friends remember that an anxious Regina kept a list of acceptable friends for her daughter and that a child who was not on the list was sent home from the O'Connor house.

On the back porch and in what was then a dirt backyard of the Charlton Street residence lived the ducks and chickens that Mary Flannery enjoyed, one of which was the "frizzled" chicken (so named because its feathers grow backward) that she taught to walk backward. That chicken was the subject of a brief spot on Pathé News in the late 1920s; the child Mary Flannery is pictured with her chicken in a delightful vignette, now available for viewing in the O'Connor Collection of Georgia College & State University in Milledgeville. And just why did O'Connor have chickens as pets, and not the customary dogs and cats? Some relatives recall that the child was deathly afraid of cats and dogs, while others suggest that Regina O'Connor was fearful that Mary Flannery would pick up germs. In any case, to the end of her life, fowl would continue to be a part of O'Connor's domestic environment, the best-known birds of all being the numerous peacocks at the Milledgeville farm Andalusia, with which the author is so frequently associated.

Mary Flannery's childhood bedroom

Living room, with photograph of
Mrs. Raphael Semmes on the table

By all accounts, Mary Flannery O'Connor had a strict and protected childhood. Savannah friends recall that, although her father doted on her, the two were rarely seen in public together. In fact, the Charlton Street household was the beginning of the strongly matriarchal society that would surround the writer throughout her formative years.

O'Connor's Community

Mary Flannery entered St. Vincent's Grammar School for Girls in 1931; the school, which was run by the Sisters of Mercy, provided a highly disciplined atmosphere for the young Catholic children in the neighborhood. Regina O'Connor walked her daughter the short distance to St. Vincent's, located just across the street in a large, roomy house next to the Cathedral

St. Vincent's Grammar School for Girls, Mary Flannery's first parochial school (1931–36). Courtesy of the Georgia Historical Society

Sacred Heart Grammar School, Mary Flannery's second parochial school. Courtesy of the Georgia Historical Society

of St. John the Baptist. (A church office building has replaced the school). At St. Vincent's young Mary Flannery was instructed in the Baltimore Catechism (asked the same questions, of course, as Father Finn puts to Asbury in "The Enduring Chill") and in the tenets of her faith.

For the school year of 1936–37 Mary Flannery transferred to Sacred Heart Grammar School (no longer standing), located on Abercorn Street some distance from her home. She was driven there by Regina O'Connor in Cousin Katie's electric car; her classmates remember eagerly awaiting the arrival of the car each afternoon. Mary Flannery's teachers there were the Sisters of St. Joseph of Corondolet. The reasons for O'Connor's transferring are not clear, although some friends and relatives suggest that the strictness of the nuns at St. Vincent's might have been a factor. Others posit that Sacred Heart had a stronger educational reputation than St. Vincent's and was a bit more genteel than the neighborhood school. In any event, while at Sacred Heart, Mary Flannery joined the Girl Scouts, and continued her drawing, writing, and voracious reading, often making notes on the flyleaves of books; on Lewis Carroll's *Alice's Adventures in Wonderland* she wrote, "Awful. I wouldn't read this book," on Shirley Watkins's *Georgina Finds Herself*, "This is the worst book I ever read next to 'Pinnochio,'" and on Louisa May Alcott's *Little Men*, "First rate, splendid." Evidently the young writer had little use for fantasy.

In the summers Regina and Mary Flannery often visited Regina's birthplace and childhood home in Milledgeville, where Mary Flannery came to know her various Cline relatives and to enjoy leisurely summers in the middle-Georgia town where she would eventually make her home. At age ten Mary Flannery wrote and illustrated a little book called "My Relatives," evincing her delight in the eccentricity of her large family.

In her essay "The Nature and Aim of Fiction," Flannery O'Connor asserts that any writer "who has survived his childhood has enough information about life to last him the rest of his days." In this statement O'Connor is not referring necessarily to those dramatic episodes that

"Sister Perpetua, the oldest nun at the Sisters of Mercy in Mayville, had given them a lecture on what to do if a young man should—here they laughed so hard they were not able to go on without going back to the beginning—on what to do if a young man should—they put their heads in their laps—on what to do if—they finally managed to shout it out—if he should 'behave in an ungentlemanly manner in the back seat of an automobile.' Sister Perpetua said they were to say 'Stop, sir! I am a Temple of the Holy Ghost!'" ("A Temple of the Holy Ghost")

often punctuate, if not puncture, our early years but simply to the truths etched on the human heart in that formative time. O'Connor was an only child in a devoutly Catholic family in a devoutly Catholic community, but even in such a homogeneous and protected setting, she absorbed many of life's profound lessons. For example, her mother sometimes took her to visit St. Mary's Home in Savannah, an orphanage for girls run by the nuns. In a letter to her friend Betty Hester near the end of her life, O'Connor writes, "When I was a child [the orphanage] was in a creaking house on a dreary street and I was occasionally taken there to visit the Sisters or some orphan distant-cousins; also probably as a salutary lesson. 'See what you have to be thankful for. Suppose you were, etc.'—a lesson my imagination played on exhaustively." Later in that same letter she adds, "I have been at least an Imaginary Orphan and that was probably my first view of Hell. Children know by instinct that Hell is an absence of love."

The reader of O'Connor's fiction may easily remember the vast loneliness of such young characters as Norton in "The Lame Shall Enter First," Harry/Bevel in "The River," and even the unattractive but wise Mary Fortune Pitts in "A View of the Woods." A strong and recurrent theme in all of O'Connor's work is the hellish barrenness of a child's loveless life and what that child may do to compensate for such a lack. It might well be argued, by extension, that the important theme of displacement, in all of the ways in which it is manifested in the fiction, is integrally related to the theme of lovelessness: after all, in O'Connor's view, through original sin and the Fall, we were all *displaced*, orphaned and estranged from God's love. Only by means of the grace afforded us by Christ's suffering, death, and resurrection are we able to experience—through faith—a restoration of right relationship to God, to become again the children of God and rightful heirs to His kingdom. Thus, although Flannery O'Connor experienced a loving, caring childhood, she was early on able to perceive what life without Love is like.

The Cathedral of St. John the Baptist

Just across the square from the childhood home is the formidable Cathedral of St. John the Baptist, where Mary Flannery O'Connor was baptized on April 12, 1925, where she made her First Communion on May 8, 1932, and where she was confirmed on May 20, 1934.

Savannah's first parish, the Congregation de Saint Jean-Baptiste, was established by French Catholic settlers in the late eighteenth century. On May 30, 1799, the mayor and aldermen of Savannah reserved half a trust lot on Liberty Square for the congregation's use, and one year later the small frame church of St. John the Baptist was built. The parish grew, and in 1835 a larger church was built between Perry and McDonough to replace the original building. Its congregation included about one-third of the entire Catholic population of Georgia.

Since 1820 Georgia had been a part of the Diocese of Charleston. Not until 1850 was the Diocese of Savannah established by Pope Pius IX; it would include all of Georgia and most of Florida. The Church of St. John the Baptist then became the cathedral and was at the time the only Catholic church in Savannah. In 1870, the diocese covered only the state of Georgia and consisted of thirty churches and some twenty thousand Catholics. At this time, the fourth bishop of Savannah, the Right Reverend Ignatius Persico, developed plans for the building of a new cathedral. The cathedral was dedicated by the Most Reverend James Roosevelt Bayley, archbishop of Baltimore, on April 30, 1876. With the building of the spires in 1896, the French Gothic cathedral was finally complete. The impressive nave and transepts were complemented by bronze-colored iron columns supporting triple rows of arches. The main and side altars were white Italian marble. There was certainly no structure so grand in the entire state.

St. John the Baptist Cathedral, present day

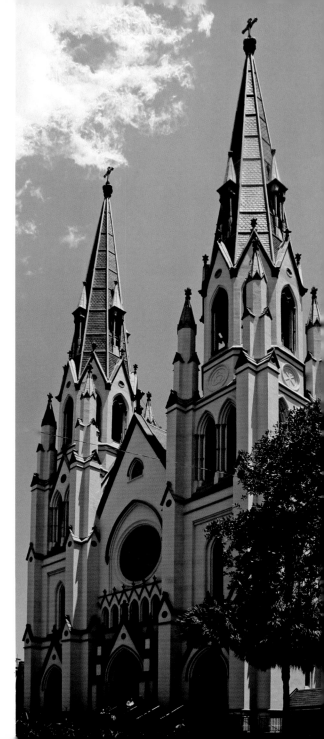

Baptismal font and sanctuary

But tragedy struck. On February 6, 1898, the cathedral was nearly destroyed by fire, as thousands watched. Except for the bishop's residence and the outside walls and two spires, nothing remained standing. Immediately, plans were made to rebuild, and on December 24, 1899, the Right Reverend Benjamin Keiley presided over the first Mass in the rebuilt cathedral, in the basement chapel.

Following its rededication in 1900, the cathedral was redecorated: murals, planned and directed in their painting by respected Savannah artist Christopher Murphy, were installed, as were stained glass windows, depicting the life of St. John the Baptist, the Ascension of Christ, and the Assumption of the Blessed Virgin Mary. The rose window is a quatrefoil featuring St. Cecilia, the patron saint of music, at its center; heavenly figures singing and playing musical instruments radiate from that center.

Visitors may be interested in knowing that the last window on the cathedral's right side was part of the original cathedral. The "new" windows were created by the Innsbruck Glassmakers in the Austrian Tyrol. The stations of the cross, which are important to Catholics as they relive the Passion of Christ, are richly colored Bavarian woodcarvings. The bishop's chair, the cathedra, was also added at this time. Formally reopened in 1912, the cathedral was consecrated in 1920, an event that could occur in those days only when the church was debt-free. The baptismal font and the main altar both were installed in 2000. The font, carved in Carrara, Italy, features at its center a Celtic knot, the Irish symbol for eternity, and, in Latin, the words of John the Baptist: "He who sent me to baptize with water, He it is Who Baptizes with the Holy Spirit."

Other renovations occurred in the years between 1959 and 1963, including the addition of the wide plaza at the entrance and the installation of modern heating, cooling, and lighting systems. The colors in the church were modified to resemble the colors prior to the 1898 fire. In 1987 the Noack tracker organ, made entirely of white oak and trimmed in black walnut, was installed. More significantly, and in keeping with the liturgi-

Celtic knot inside the baptismal font

cal changes of Vatican II, in the 1980s the high altar came to be used as a backdrop, while at a new altar the priest faced the congregation for the first time in the history of the church. The new main altar bears in Latin the inscription "Blessed are they who have been called to the supper of the Lamb," reminding the visitor of the central importance of the Eucharist to Flannery O'Connor.

One hundred years after the terrible fire, in 1998, the Most Reverend J. Kevin Boland, the thirteenth bishop of Savannah, called for a major renovation of the cathedral, to be directed by the Reverend William O. O'Neill. This renovation involved the removal, cleaning, and re-leading of more than fifty stained glass windows, replacing of the slate roof, and refurbishing of the interior. In November 2000 the project was completed, just in time to celebrate the one-hundred-and-fiftieth anniversary of the

"The child knelt down between her mother and the nun and they were well into the '*Tantum Ergo*' before her ugly thoughts stopped and she began to realize that she was in the presence of God. Hep me not to be so mean, she began mechanically. Hep me not to give her so much sass. Hep me not to talk like I do." ("A Temple of the Holy Ghost")

Savannah Diocese and the one-hundredth anniversary of the rededication of the cathedral in 1900.

In 2003 an arsonist destroyed the pulpit, just to the right of the main altar; an exact replica of that pulpit, featuring carvings of the four evangelists, replaced the burned one.

This impressive church, then, was the religious center of the early life of Mary Flannery O'Connor, who was, by all accounts, a dutiful and devout child, if not at times a bit of a social renegade. Who can begin to account for the impression made by this vast and beautiful sanctuary on the mind of a sensitive and God-fearing child? O'Connor's somewhat autobiographical story "A Temple of the Holy Ghost" surely testifies to both the desire of the child to please God and the power of the sacraments to aid in the achievement of goodness. At the conclusion of this story, when the crucifix hanging from the nun's belt is mashed into the child's face as the nun hugs her, we may indeed sense the imprint of Christ on the heart of one of O'Connor's most honest and appealing characters.

O'Connor never rebelled against the strictures of the Church, though it is clear that in her childhood, as in the case of many a Catholic child, particular nuns were capable of giving her grief. It is equally clear that Mary Flannery received a firm grounding in church teachings that would sustain her throughout her life.

"'I preach there are all kinds of truth, your truth and somebody else's, but behind all of them, there's only one truth and that is that there's no truth,' he called. 'No truth behind all truths is what I and this church preach! Where you come from is gone, where you thought you were going to never was there, and where you are is no good unless you can get away from it. Where is there a place for you to be? No place.'" (*Wise Blood*)

Milledgeville

LITTLE DID MARY FLANNERY O'CONNOR imagine that the large, comfortable Cline family home on Greene Street in Milledgeville, which she had visited each summer in her childhood, would become her home from 1938 to 1945, when she graduated from Georgia State College for Women.

Ed O'Connor had moved his family to Atlanta in 1938 where they lived in a house (no longer standing) at 2525 Potomac Avenue and where for a brief time Mary Flannery attended North Fulton High School, her first experience of public school. Regina and Mary Flannery lived in Atlanta for over a year, but city life was not to their liking. The two moved to Regina's family home in Milledgeville, and Ed O'Connor drove down on weekends to visit. While in Atlanta, however, Ed became ill with systemic lupus erythematosus, and he joined his wife and daughter in Milledgeville, where he died three years later, in 1941. He was buried in Milledgeville in Memory Hill Cemetery, only two blocks from the Cline family home; Mary Flannery O'Connor was fifteen years old.

Ed O'Connor's death was a grievous blow to his wife and daughter, who was then attending Peabody High School. In all likelihood because of the loss of her father, Mary Flannery remained in Milledgeville for her college years at GSCW. Again, in 1950, some years after O'Connor had completed her MFA at the State University of Iowa, she found herself in Milledgeville, ill with the same disease that had killed her father and dependent on her mother's watchful eye. Milledgeville, Georgia, thus looms large in the life

"My standard is: When in Rome, do as you done in Milledgeville." (*The Habit of Being*)

"My idea about Atlanta is get in, get it over with and get out before dark." (*The Habit of Being*)

"The stores in Taulkinham stayed open on Thursday nights so that people could have an extra opportunity to see what was for sale." (*Wise Blood*)

OPPOSITE: *The Gordon-Porter-Ward-Beall-Cline-O'Connor-Florencourt House*

Milledgeville

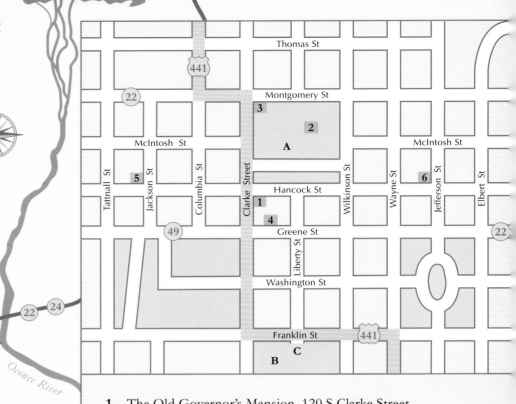

Andalusia Farm
2628 N Columbia St
Highway 441 N

N

441

212

22

22 24

Downtown

Oconee River

49

441

112

243

Central State Hospital
620 Broad Street

Thomas St

441

22

Montgomery St

3

2

McIntosh St

A

McIntosh St

Tattnall St

Jackson St

Columbia St

Clarke Street

5

Wilkinson St

Wayne St

Jefferson St

Elbert St

6

Hancock St

1

49

4

Greene St

Liberty St

22

Washington St

Franklin St 441

C

B

1. The Old Governor's Mansion, 120 S Clarke Street

2. Peabody High School, formerly on the campus of GCSU

3. The Flannery O'Connor Collection,
   Ina Dillard Russell Library, GCSU campus

4. The Gordon-Porter-Ward-Beall-Cline-O'Connor-
   Florencourt House

5. The Brown-Stetson-Sanford House, 601 W Hancock Street

6. Sacred Heart Church, 110 N Jefferson Street

A. Georgia State College for Women
   (now Georgia College & State University)

B. Memory Hill Cemetery

C. Entrance to Memory Hill Cemetery

and work of Flannery O'Connor. She spent her most productive writing years here.

Following her recovery from the initial and nearly fatal attack of the disease in 1950–51, Flannery O'Connor gradually grew accustomed to the idea that Milledgeville was to be her permanent home. She accommodated herself to the rhythms of small-town existence and to life in central Georgia. In fact, Milledgeville would become at least a humorous benchmark for O'Connor's standards of deportment and savoir faire; she averred that her motto was "When in Rome, do as you done in Milledgeville," a town so remote that it can be reached, she wrote, "only by bus or by buzzard."

Certainly Milledgeville and life in a small southern town lent themselves to O'Connor's satiric eye; in admonishing one friend to return soon from

The Oconee River at Milledgeville

Japan, she advocated a return to the "Bird Sanctuary, where all is culture, graciousness, refinement and bidnis-like common sense." She wrote to that same friend that when she was forced to return to the South, "I was roped and tied and resigned the way it is necessary to be resigned to death and largely because I thought it would be the end of any creation, any writing, any work from me." However, what she discovered, to her surprise and relief, was that her return South was "only the beginning" of her work. It is safe to say that, although O'Connor's actual physical distance from the centers of literary culture was bound to be frustrating at times, O'Connor came to delight in her quasi-rural life and to find within it source material that well suited her aims. Indeed, most commentators believe that O'Connor's forced return to Milledgeville may have provided the most fertile environment for her fiction. Like Faulkner in his significant return to that "postage-stamp" of land he knew well in Mississippi, O'Connor found in this central Georgia community ample material for her writing. Her friend Sally Fitzgerald liked to say that, in Milledgeville, "Flannery was like a silver miner at the Comstock Lode."

The city of Milledgeville, on the west bank of the Oconee River, was formally established in 1803 on land ceded by the Creek Indians in an 1802 treaty. Before the city's establishment, the territory had been the site of ongoing struggles among settlers, Indians, and federal troops assigned to the region by President George Washington to maintain peace between the frontiersmen and the natives.

In 1804 the state legislature declared Milledgeville to be the seat of government, and so it remained until 1868, three years after the end of the Civil War. Earlier state capitals were Savannah, Augusta, and Louisville, but as the frontier moved steadily westward, a more centrally located seat of government was deemed necessary. Milledgeville, planned and laid out in squares to accommodate its role as capital of Georgia, was named in honor of John Milledge, governor from 1802 to 1806. The town contained sixteen lots, each of 202 $^1/_2$ acres, totaling 3,240 acres. Only a small portion

"At six o'clock in the morning I heard the following conversation from two nurses in the hall. What have you done with them sheets? I ain't done nothing with them. Well I tole you what to do with them. You ain't never done no suchofva thing. I know what I done. I know what you done too. You may know what you done but you don't know what I done. This went on for some time. It was the first vacation my mother has had in years, this being in the hospital for a week." (*The Habit of Being*)

of the land—in one-acre lots—was designated as residential. By 1807 the statehouse, now the central building on the campus of Georgia Military College, was far enough along in its construction to allow the legislature to meet there, though the building was not completed until 1811.

The Old Governor's Mansion

Once the residence of Georgia's governors, the Old Governor's Mansion on Clarke Street is perhaps the most widely photographed building in Georgia. However, this fine home was preceded by Government House, a far less elegant home for the state's governors at the same location as the Mansion. On two lots of an acre apiece on Clarke Street between Hancock and Greene, Government House, a two-story frame structure that became increasingly dilapidated, served as the residence of Georgia's governors until 1839, when the Mansion was completed. Built during the tenure of Governor William Schley, the Mansion was planned by three architects—John Pell, C. B. Clusky, and H. A. Norris. Clusky's design was the final version chosen and was built at a cost of fifty thousand dollars. Timothy Porter, a builder from Farmington, Connecticut, was chiefly responsible for the final appearance of the Mansion. In fact, the building was largely a work of "Yankee" workmanship, as few local artisans were hired. The regal building was patterned in the High Greek Revival style, which exemplified America's respect for the birthplace of democracy. Although there is no balcony outside, there is an impressive rotunda and balcony inside. The salon is over sixty feet long and is patterned after the East Room of the White House. In the years preceding the Civil War, the Mansion became the center of Milledgeville social life and the state's political headquarters.

Milledgeville was a center of activity during the Civil War. In 1861 the Secession Convention met here and, three days after convening, voted to secede. Several volunteer military units in support of the Confederate cause

The Governor's Mansion, 1955.
Courtesy, The Old Governor's
Mansion, GCSU

were formed here, the oldest of which was the Baldwin Blues. Although some citizens did not support secession, most supported the war effort. Before it was all over, of course, Milledgeville itself came under attack. In 1864 a detachment of Union horsemen from George Stoneman's cavalry raiders threatened the city, and, finally, General William Tecumseh Sherman invaded, destroying several homes, the central depot, the bridge across the Oconee River, and the state arsenal. However, when the damage is compared with that of other southern cities attacked by Sherman, Milledgeville can be said to have fared rather well.

Complete restoration of the Old Governor's Mansion was begun in 2001, following some seven years of preparatory archival work and actual physical investigation of the building to determine the scope and depth of the project. With a price tag of $9.5 million, the restoration took some three years to complete. The Mansion officially reopened in 2005. This beautiful

The restored Governor's Mansion, GCSU, present day

restored building, complete with outbuildings and bookstore, has been recognized by the National Trust for Historic Preservation and is hailed by some Georgians as the most important building in the state. Today, the Mansion serves as a Historic House Museum. Due to the breadth of its social and political history, the Mansion was designated a National Historic Landmark Building in 1973.

In spite of the presence of this fine centerpiece of southern history in her midst, Flannery O'Connor was never interested in Civil War history as a primary subject for her fiction; in only one story, "A Late Encounter with the Enemy," does she use the "Wah Between the States," as she humorously called it. In that story, moreover, O'Connor is intent on poking fun at the sentimental myths about the Old South and the war and at the foolishly worshipful devotion many die-hard southerners give the Confederate cause. "A Late Encounter" is also the only O'Connor story that takes place on the campus of GSCW; O'Connor's material is an altered version of the actual appearance in Russell Auditorium of "General" William J. Bush of Fitzgerald, Georgia, dressed in his Confederate uniform to honor the graduation of his sixty-two-year-old wife.

In her fictional restaging of this event, O'Connor suggests that many so-called unreconstructed southerners resemble her protagonist, "General" Sash, who has fabricated his war experience and who, dressed in a general's uniform, is dragged in his senility from one Confederate memorial to another, to demonstrate the pride of the Cause. It is doubtful that the "General" ever understood the meaning of his experience or the significance of the tragic "fall" of the South. O'Connor, like Walker Percy, believed that the defeat of the South in the War led to a heightened sense of place for the best of southern writers, including, of course, William Faulkner, Eudora Welty, and Robert Penn Warren. As she says in a letter to a friend in the North, "I think you have a sense of place up there, but since it is not connected with a historical defeat, I don't think it touches as deep an emotion. . . . It's not simply a matter of present-place, but a

"Every year on Confederate Memorial Day, he was bundled up and lent to the Capitol City Museum where he was displayed from one to four in a musty room full of old photographs, old uniforms, old artillery, and historic documents. All these were carefully preserved in glass cases so that children would not put their hands on them. He wore his general's uniform from the premiere and sat, with a fixed scowl, inside a small roped area." ("A Late Encounter with the Enemy")

matter of the place's continuity and the shared experience of the people who live there."

In all likelihood, O'Connor eschewed the Civil War as subject matter at least partly because of the precedent of Georgian Margaret Mitchell's *Gone with the Wind*, published in 1936 to great popular, if not literary, acclaim. O'Connor was only eleven years old at the time, but the continued and widespread popularity of the book through the years, coupled with the romantic movie version of it that appeared in 1939, would have turned the tough-minded, unsentimental O'Connor in quite another direction. O'Connor was, furthermore, educated to be what would be called, in today's unfortunate parlance, a literary writer, not necessarily a popular one. O'Connor's work is deliberately aimed at a rather sophisticated audience, one whose reading and understanding would enable it to grasp irony and to delight in the comic use of the grotesque. Thus, while Margaret Mitchell might have delighted in the life associated with the Old Governor's Mansion, O'Connor never could. In fact, one might posit that O'Connor's fiction may be read on one level as a conscious response to the romanticism of Margaret Mitchell.

With the establishment in the late nineteenth century of Georgia Normal and Industrial College, now Georgia College & State University, the Old Governor's Mansion was renovated to provide over thirty dormitory rooms. However, the structure eventually became the home of the new college's president and the center of college social activity. Milledgeville's visitors and honored guests were usually feted in the Mansion or on its grounds, and such was the case when O'Connor returned to Milledgeville in 1950, in what became her permanent return to the area. Later in that decade and early in the 1960s, O'Connor had occasion to visit the Mansion frequently.

Flannery O'Connor's friendship with the eccentric Maryat Lee, sister of college president Robert E. "Buzz" Lee (1956–67) who lived with his family in the Mansion, provided O'Connor with many an opportunity to poke fun at what she believed to be the sometimes pretentious social life in Milledgeville. Such occasions, most of which were formal, were not among her favorites, especially when she herself was being honored. One can imagine that the polite exchanges of pleasantries and superficial conversations were simply grist for the mill of her imagination. In 1957, for example, O'Connor writes a friend, "I am getting some award from GSCW that I have to say two pages of thanksgiving for but that should be no terrible burden except that I also have to go to a coffee and a tea for it and shake innumerable paws. These things are fine for the people that like them and the people that don't, as my mother tells me, are just peculiar." For a young woman to be described, even humorously, as being "peculiar" in the midfifties was tantamount to saying that she had stepped well outside the boundaries of the expected female behavior of her social class. Flannery O'Connor never minded being so considered; in fact, she even reveled in her disdain for such superficial engagements.

The Cline House

The house at 311 W. Greene Street, where Flannery O'Connor lived from 1938 until her departure for Iowa City in 1945, is one of Milledgeville's most important historic homes. When the House of Representatives met in 1838, it authorized a home to be rented for use by the governor until the Mansion was completed and ready to be occupied. The home selected for the first and second years was the same house, belonging in 1838 to H. P. Ward and in 1839 to Jeremiah Beall (thus the Ward-Beall-Cline House, as it once was known). Soon after the Civil War the home was purchased by Peter James Cline, Flannery O'Connor's grandfather. It has remained in the Cline family since that time.

With solid front columns that were handcarved by slaves, the Cline House stands on the southern side of what was then called Mansion Square. The four front rooms of the house, upstairs and down, were part

"As for biographies, there won't be any biographies of me because, for only one reason, lives spent between the house and the chicken yard do not make exciting copy." (*The Habit of Being*)

of the original structure. A "candle lamp" chandelier hangs in the front hall, and in the drawing room is an antique concert grand piano. The Clines and their relatives and friends experienced many happy times in this large and accommodating house. Mary Flannery enjoyed a second-floor bedroom and used the attic space of the third floor as her drawing studio during her high school and college years. Neighbors from those days recalled Mary Flannery in her early teens sitting in the swing with her feathered friends, often dressed in the clothes she had made them, on the extended porch (added in the late 1900s and removed in the 1980s to restore historical accuracy). The handsome open-worked brick wall surrounding much of the property was originally made of handmade bricks; at the time of its construction, the wall enclosed the entire block.

Georgia College & State University and Peabody High School

Known as Georgia State College for Women in O'Connor's time, Georgia College & State University has undergone a number of changes in name and mission over the years since its founding as Georgia Normal and Industrial College in 1891. Established as the female industrial school of the state and, originally, as part of the University of Georgia, the two-year college was funded with thirty-five thousand dollars from the state legislature, half of what the initial appropriation had called for. To make up the difference, Georgia Military College was to relinquish the Old Governor's Mansion and Penitentiary Square (which consisted of twenty acres) for use by the female college.

Although the establishment of the college was greeted with skepticism on the part of some local citizens, among whom was a local editor who argued that the value of the military college far outweighed the value of a "Girls Industrial School," the town was generally willing to invest in it. Local bonds were passed to assist the building program. From this money,

Betty Boyd Love and Mary Flannery O'Connor on the steps of Lanier Hall at Georgia State College for Women, 1944. Courtesy, Flannery O'Connor Collection, GCSU Library

Atkinson Hall, built in 1896, was used as a dormitory for GSCW and included a dining room with kitchen facilities when O'Connor attended school there.

some five thousand dollars was spent on the Mansion, which was repaired and partitioned into thirty-five dormitory rooms. Old Main, the first classroom building, was completed in 1891. The first president, J. Harris Chappell, along with Julia Flisch, a bold and forward-looking member of the faculty, envisioned a school with an egalitarian atmosphere where there would be no monetary or class distinctions among the female students. At the inauspicious opening of the college in September of 1891, there were eighty-eight students. By the end of that first year there were 171; by the end of the first decade, there were four hundred young women enrolled.

The charter of Georgia Normal and Industrial College required that all students be instructed in at least one of the "industrial arts," including cooking, typing, bookkeeping, telegraphy, and dressmaking, though there was also some attention paid to the liberal arts. The young women lived under careful surveillance and were rarely allowed to visit town, only one block from the campus. Male companionship was frowned upon in the early days of the school, although, as might be expected, the cadets at GMC and young men from Mercer University in Macon sometimes boldly challenged that prohibition.

The reputation of the college increased throughout the southeast in the following years, and, finally in 1922, under the astute leadership of President Marvin Parks, the school was separated from the control of the University of Georgia, renamed Georgia State College for Women, and allowed to grant four-year degrees. In 1932, GSCW became a part of the University System of Georgia, governed by the Board of Regents. Under the leadership of President Guy H. Wells, enrollment at the college reached its peak in 1938 at fifteen hundred women, just before Mary Flannery O'Connor was about to enroll. Many of the local students had received their high school education at Peabody High School, the laboratory school at the college, as had Mary Flannery.

For years an important part of GSCW, Peabody High School (no longer standing), administered through the Department of Education at the col-

Lanier Hall, constructed in 1925, was used as a classroom building for GSCW. A later addition behind the hall housed Peabody High School, where O'Connor was a student.

lege, was established as a practicum for high school teachers when Georgia Normal and Industrial College initiated its teacher education program in 1891. Two purposes were served by the establishment of the school: to provide a "normal school" education to young girls and to train the young female students at the college to become teachers, with a master teacher in each area supporting the student teachers. The male counterpart to Peabody High School was Georgia Military College, although occasionally a male student who refused to attend a military school would be enrolled in Peabody. In the lower grades, there were boys and girls in each school. When Baldwin High School was established in 1927, Peabody's enrollment began to decrease.

For Mary Flannery O'Connor, who had in her early years been educated at parochial schools, the Peabody experience proved salutary. When her family moved to Milledgeville in 1938, after almost two years in Atlanta, she enrolled in the eighth grade at Peabody, on the northern side of the GSCW campus, scarcely a three-block walk from the Cline family residence. The curriculum at Peabody was called "experimental," for it was one of ten Georgia schools selected by the state to participate in a state-coordinated curriculum, for which the teachers were answerable to the government. O'Connor, in contrast to many of her classmates in their enthusiasm for Peabody, later criticized the subject matter taught, complaining that she was not instructed in the classics. Throughout her life, O'Connor expressed little but disdain for John Dewey and his progressivism, which, in her opinion, allowed weak and undisciplined students to remain dilettantes. O'Connor's brief essay "Total Effect and the Eighth Grade" is a fierce attack on curricula that are approved or vetoed by students themselves: "No one asks the student if algebra pleases him or if he finds it satisfactory that some French verbs are irregular, but if he prefers [John] Hersey to Hawthorne, his taste must prevail." She goes on to argue that students' taste should not be consulted, for "it is being formed."

"Then Mr. Head explained the sewer system, how the entire city was underlined with it, how it contained all the drainage and was full of rats and how a man could slide into it and be sucked along down endless pitchblack tunnels. At any minute any man in the city might be sucked into the sewer and never heard from again."
("The Artificial Nigger")

Nevertheless, at Peabody Mary Flannery felt at least free enough to continue working on her cartoons and to write for the school newspaper, the *Peabody Palladium*. In the experimental home economics class, when she was asked to make an apron for herself, she sewed clothes for her pet duck. Her teacher accepted the substitution, reasoning that more skill with the needle was required in making duck clothes than in making an apron. Another teacher recalled a dinner at the Cline house where she met Mary Flannery's pet duck Henry, who, after depositing an egg, was renamed Henrietta. That story was recounted in young Mary Flannery's homemade book, "Mistaken Identity," which early demonstrated her ability as writer and illustrator. A copy of the book is now available in the O'Connor Collection at Georgia College & State University.

In her second year at Peabody, Mary Flannery became art editor for the newspaper and contributed poems, book reviews, and satiric sketches, many of which are in the O'Connor Collection at GCSU. She continued her literary and artistic activity throughout the Peabody years, and in her senior year O'Connor won a prize in a statewide essay contest sponsored by Rich's department store in Atlanta. An article about O'Connor in the *Palladium* in 1941 records O'Connor saying that she had begun writing at the age of six and had already produced three books, each about a goose. The article clearly reveals a young girl with decided opinions, a strong personality, and unconventional interests, including her pet fowl—Hallie Selassie, her pet rooster; Winston, a black crow; and the deceased Adolph, another rooster whose name had to be changed because of its obvious political liability at that time. O'Connor's sly sense of humor was evident to her classmates at Peabody. During the Peabody years she also submitted her Thurber-like cartoons to the *New Yorker*, receiving her first rejection slips.

In the summer following her graduation from Peabody High School in 1942, in the year following the entry of the United States into World War II, Mary Flannery entered Georgia State College for Women, enrolling as a day student in an accelerated three-year program. Most Peabody graduates went on to attend GSCW (to become Jessies, as they were nicknamed), where they knew many of the professors already. Furthermore, in the war years when O'Connor attended, money for higher education was scarce, and few could afford to travel elsewhere for an education. Mary Flannery O'Connor was no exception to this fact, for her family enjoyed only a modest income. The Peabody graduate, however, had an additional reason for remaining at home—the death of her beloved father. Thus, for her college years O'Connor lived at home with Regina and other family members and walked over to the campus for her classes and extracurricular activities.

Georgia State College for Women was then known as a teachers' college, if not as *the* teachers' college of the state. The institution attracted young women from throughout the state who received, if not a classical education, at least exposure to a well-rounded curriculum in an atmosphere that allowed them the intellectual freedom that many educators believed was not possible for females in a coeducational environment. Although O'Connor complained in later years about her undergraduate education and claimed that she had never read much of anything when she graduated, she was able to continue developing her talents as writer and cartoonist at GSCW. Majoring in social sciences, with a minor in English, O'Connor was taught by some fine teachers. One of them, in particular, Hallie Smith, appreciated O'Connor's wit and her talent, encouraging her to contribute to the literary magazine, the *Corinthian*. O'Connor was a prolific contributor to that magazine, serving as editor her senior year; she continued her cartooning, and her work was displayed on the walls of the student coffee shop (long since painted over) in the basement of Parks Hall, as well as in the yearbook, the literary magazine, and the college newspaper, the *Colonnade*. O'Connor's nonfiction, poetry, and fiction at this time were marked by the satiric wit, exaggeration, and delight in the bizarre that would characterize the mature work.

The years of O'Connor's attendance at GSCW were unusual in that the college had been declared a wartime clerical training center for Navy storekeepers, and, as a result, contingents of WAVES—Women Accepted for Volunteer Emergency Service—encamped in Milledgeville and on the campus. After their arrival in February of 1943, the college newspaper carried photographs of the WAVES marching on campus, including in front of the Mansion, and making up their military bunks. Because of the presence of the WAVES, Bob Hope brought his USO Show to Russell Auditorium, though attendance was limited to only Naval Training School personnel and GSCW students. Some local historians actually claim to see Flannery O'Connor's face in photographs of the show, though there is no evidence, to date, that she attended the event.

O'Connor used the presence of the WAVES as the subject of many of her woodcut cartoons, which were published in the literary magazine and college yearbook. From poking fun at the obliviousness of the WAVES to their student counterparts; to an image suggesting that students wonder, as they see a WAVE searching her briefcase, if she's looking for gunpowder; to a student archer aiming bow and arrow at the marching women, O'Connor had a great time with the WAVES. This lightly satirical treatment may be viewed, indeed, as a rather bold move on the part of a college undergraduate, especially in a time of war when all efforts on the home front were taken very seriously. Surely O'Connor's temerity is a portent of her style and subject matter in the mature, published work: she is never afraid to go against the grain of the acceptable. In fact, rebellion against conventional attitudes is a hallmark of her fiction, which she intended to jolt the reader; as she later wrote, "For the hard of hearing you shout; for the almost blind, you draw large and startling figures." To be sure, the comic exaggeration of her cartoons is soon to be channeled into the sharp visual imagery of her stories and novels. O'Connor's use of the grotesque, her dark humor, and her habit of turning fictional expectations inside out are surely forecast in the writing and drawings of her college years.

"The black procession wound its way up the two blocks and started on the main walk leading to the auditorium. The visitors stood on the grass, picking out their graduates. Men were pushing back their hats and wiping their foreheads and women were lifting their dresses slightly from the shoulders to keep them from sticking to their backs. The graduates in their heavy robes looked as if the last beads of ignorance were being sweated out of them." ("A Late Encounter with the Enemy")

Russell Auditorium, constructed in 1928, was the facility used for most large events involving the entire college community during O'Connor's college days.

Although O'Connor did not capitalize on Civil War material, she did, in fact, use World War II and the Holocaust as significant background in one important story, "The Displaced Person." This long story appeared in her first collection of stories, *A Good Man Is Hard to Find* (1955), and features at its center a smug, selfish, and self-centered farm widow, Mrs. McIntyre, who is initially delighted to hire a displaced Pole and his family to work on her farm: "One fellow's misery is another fellow's gain," she says. Mr. Guizac, the Pole, is able to work miracles on the farm, and Mrs. McIntyre is pleased—until she discovers the Pole's plan to rescue a cousin from a concentration camp and marry her to "one of [her] Negroes." Viewing others solely in terms of their usefulness to her and, in that way, ultimately denying their humanity, Mrs. McIntyre is finally complicit in the murder of the displaced person; she herself, then, is displaced, both physically and spiritually. O'Connor makes frequent reference in this story to images of boxcars and fragmented, broken bodies as though to underscore the dehumanizing outlook of the Mrs. McIntyres and the Hitlers of this world. The microcosm is the macrocosm, O'Connor suggests; a sense of individual or group superiority, coupled with overweening selfishness and greed, is counter to all that Christ taught of love and compassion. Herein lies the road to the gas chamber.

Upon her graduation from GSCW in 1945, O'Connor headed to the graduate program at the State University of Iowa, to which a philosophy teacher at GSCW had encouraged her to apply. Initially, she entered as a graduate student in journalism; her immediate distaste for that program, however, led her to approach Paul Engle, director of the newly instituted Writers' Workshop, and ask to be admitted to the graduate creative writing program. After he had read samples of her work, Engle had no problem whatsoever in admitting O'Connor, who became, after her two years in the MFA program there, one of its most distinguished graduates. Her graduate thesis was a collection of short stories entitled *The Geranium and Other Stories*. While at Iowa and during some postgraduate work there, O'Connor did much of the writing of *Wise Blood*, her first novel. Clearly, Georgia State College for Women had well equipped Flannery O'Connor for her graduate education, in spite of her protests to the contrary.

In 1961, largely as the result of the efforts of President Robert E. Lee, who readily defended the cause of female education, the college was again renamed: The Woman's College of Georgia. There is no recorded reaction of Flannery O'Connor to this name change. Three years after O'Connor's death the Board of Regents pressured the college to become coeducational, arguing that its facilities were not being fully used. In 1967 the first male students were admitted, and the institution was renamed Georgia College. However, still further changes were afoot.

In the 1980s, under the leadership of President Edwin G. Speir, it appeared that the college would become a regional university. Nevertheless,

Mary Flannery O'Connor as a senior at GSCW, 1945. Courtesy, Flannery O'Connor Collection, GCSU Library

OPPOSITE: *One of Mary Flannery O'Connor's typewriters*

in 1995 the mission of the college changed suddenly and radically. The institution became the public liberal arts university of Georgia, to provide at a fraction of the cost the same high-caliber educational experience available at private colleges and universities. The new mission precipitated yet another new name: Georgia College & State University. The first female president in the history of the institution, Dr. Rosemary DePaolo, was inaugurated in 1996. Dr. DePaolo was followed by another female president, Dr. Dorothy Leland, in 2004.

The Flannery O'Connor Collection

The international reputation of Flannery O'Connor, the most distinguished graduate of the college, helped immensely in securing this coveted new mission among the state's schools. Also contributing strongly to the liberal arts tradition and image of the school was the Flannery O'Connor Collection, housed in Ina Dillard Russell Library, established through Regina Cline O'Connor's generous gift of the author's typescripts and memorabilia and funded by the Georgia College Alumni Association in 1971. The collection, officially opened in 1973, contains some six thousand pages of typescript drafts of O'Connor's major works, sorted and arranged by textual scholars, as well as translations of O'Connor's work into other languages, personal memorabilia, some furnishings, photographs, correspondence, and the author's private library. This fine collection has enabled GCSU to become the center of O'Connor studies in the world. The *Flannery O'Connor Bulletin*, a scholarly journal devoted to O'Connor's work and under the aegis of the Department of English, Speech, and Journalism, was established in 1972 and continues today as the *Flannery O'Connor Review*, the longest-running journal devoted to a woman writer in the United States.

The Brown-Stetson-Sanford House

After her return to Milledgeville in late 1950 and as she recuperated from her first serious bout with lupus, Flannery O'Connor settled into the regular daily routine that every disciplined writer needs for productivity. O'Connor usually attended Mass every morning, unless her health prohibited it, and returned to Andalusia for a morning of work. She worked at her typewriter until noon, at which time she and Regina O'Connor drove into town for lunch at the Sanford House Tea Room. For O'Connor, this daily noon meal was an important and necessary social event, for there mother and daughter greeted many of their Milledgeville friends, exchanging news and gossip and enjoying a fine, southern-cooked meal. Upon return to Andalusia after lunch, O'Connor rested and often received visitors later in the afternoon. Regina O'Connor carefully protected her daughter's fragile health by ensuring her afternoon rest and taking care that Flannery was not overwhelmed with visitors. This routine continued, for the most part, until the writer's final illness and death in August of 1964.

The Brown-Stetson-Sanford House, constructed in 1825, was designed by famous architect John Marlor and built for George Brown, a local plantation owner and businessman, and initially located on N. Wilkinson Street. The building is of Federal architectural style, though its large Palladian arch located in the pediment of the building is noteworthy. Originally used as a tavern, the building served as the headquarters for the Whig Party of Georgia from 1839 to 1847 and also served as the location of political gatherings, conventions, and the inaugural celebration of Governor George W. Crawford, Georgia's only Whig governor. When George Brown died in 1837, he left the building to his son John, who, with his partner Samuel Beecher, opened the State's Rights Hotel. In 1839, an advertisement appeared in Milledgeville's *Southern Recorder* stating that the owners "respectfully inform the public and their old patrons that they are refitting and furnishing the establishment anew for the approaching session of the legislature." Beecher and Brown thereby managed to attain access to Georgia's political power-brokers, for legislators and political leaders throughout the state lived and worked at the hotel during the legislative session. In 1840, in a show of support for the Whig presidential candidate William Henry Harrison, Brown and Beecher provided the hotel with two new names: the Anti–Van Buren State's Rights Hotel and the Harrison and Reform State's Rights Hotel. When Harrison was victorious in the election, the owners restored the original name.

In 1843 the State's Rights Hotel hosted an inaugural celebration for the newly elected governor of Georgia, George W. Crawford. However, by the late 1840s, the Whig Party had declined in influence, and the Democratic Party rose to ascendancy in southern politics. The hotel lost its steady customer base, and its operations ceased in 1847. The building was sold in 1855 to Donald Stetson, who converted it to a private residence. The house served as a private residence to two families for the next century.

In 1951 the private residence began perhaps its most notable transformation, becoming the Sanford House Tea Room, owned and operated by Miss Fannie White and Miss Mary Jo Thompson, and eventually achieving regional, if not national, recognition. The appellation "tea room," connoting in that time a gathering place for ladies of a certain class, is perhaps misleading, for, although the clientele was certainly genteel, the fare at this establishment was more substantial than that offered by the traditional tea room. Some of the finest examples of southern cuisine were served there at lunch each weekday. Both Miss White and Miss Thompson were close friends of Regina and Flannery O'Connor, often visiting them at Andalusia and sometimes bringing along samples of their renowned cuisine, to the great delight of mother and daughter. Some of Flannery O'Connor's favorite Sanford House dishes were fried shrimp, roast beef, shrimp salad, and peppermint pie.

Much to the disappointment of its community both near and far, the Sanford House Restaurant closed in 1966. The dishes served in this restaurant even today linger in the culinary memories of citizens of Milledgeville and beyond. The recipe for the delicious Sanford House salad dressing was for years one of Milledgeville's best-kept secrets.

In 1966 the building was rescued from demolition and moved to W. Hancock Street, where it was converted into a museum and civic center. Added to the National Register of Historic Places in 1972, The Brown-Stetson-Sanford House continues to be a part of Milledgeville's historic tours. It is now administered by the Old Capitol Museum located on the campus of Georgia Military College.

Central State Hospital

Some readers of O'Connor's fiction seek to draw a connection between O'Connor's bizarre and often grotesque characters and the residents of the state mental hospital, Central State, located just a few miles south of Milledgeville in Hardwick, Georgia. There is no indication whatsoever that O'Connor drew material from this source, although, like every resident

The Powell Building at
Central State Hospital

of Georgia, she was well aware of the existence of the institution and, of course, of the jokes made about Milledgeville and the state hospital, such as, "Oh, you're from Milledgeville! When did they let you out?"

Once the largest mental institution in the world and an important part of the economy of Baldwin County, Central State Hospital and its community were nonetheless quite separate from Milledgeville, though its medical personnel were often active in Milledgeville community affairs. In only one of her stories, "The Partridge Festival," does O'Connor use a mental institution; more importantly, perhaps, this story relies on a rendering of actual events in Milledgeville, which O'Connor bends to her own purposes and for which she provides a mental institution as the scene of the story's climax.

In the spring of 1953 Milledgeville celebrated its sesquicentennial with pageantry and re-enactments of historic events. Chief among those events, of course, was the Civil War and its attendant ambience, so loved by many die-hard southerners. The men in Milledgeville were to grow beards, for example, or to pay for a shaving permit; the women were to dress their part as Confederate dames. Violators of the rules, including those who would not buy festival badges, were to be placed in the public stocks or jailed in an outhouse. One can imagine the satiric eye of Flannery O'Connor delighting in such shenanigans.

The actual event in Milledgeville, however, was marred by the brutal murders of two of its most prominent citizens by a social pariah who held grudges against the two. After he murdered them, he killed himself. O'Connor modifies the facts in the case by presenting the outcast Singleton as found guilty in a mock trial of not buying an Azalea Festival badge in Partridge and as taking revenge ten days later by shooting five of the dignitaries and one innocent bystander at the festival. Singleton's case has captured the interest of young Calhoun, a "rebel-artist-mystic," who visits his doting great-aunts in Partridge simply to find out more about Singleton and his "heroic" rebellion against what Calhoun and his nemesis

Building, Central State Hospital, present day

and double Mary Elizabeth consider the repressive, stultifying community. As Calhoun remarks, "[Singleton] was a man of depth living among caricatures and they finally drove him mad, unleashed all his violence on themselves." Calhoun and Mary Elizabeth, who both consider themselves writers, want to capture in fiction and nonfiction, respectively, the story of a man being "crucified" by his community. The story's hilarious climax occurs at Quincy State Hospital, the mental institution to which Singleton has been taken. Suffice it to say that the two silly and ignorant young people receive their full comeuppance.

Although O'Connor never considered this story to be among her best, it does embody themes familiar to readers of her fiction—the bursting of the balloons of ego and superiority of her secular humanist protagonists. Central State Hospital or its like affords a fitting backdrop for Calhoun's and Mary Elizabeth's revelation that the "simple" townspeople are right: Singleton is "a bad bad bad man."

"The boy sat helpless while the car, as if of its own volition, turned and headed toward the entrance. The letters QUINCY STATE HOSPITAL were cut in a concrete arch which it rolled effortlessly through. 'Abandon hope all ye who enter here,' the girl murmured." ("The Partridge Festival")

Sacred Heart Catholic Church

After her return to Milledgeville in late 1950, Flannery O'Connor resumed worship at Sacred Heart Catholic Church on the corner of Jefferson and Hancock streets in the heart of the town. Unless ill health prevented her, O'Connor attended Mass daily.

O'Connor's maternal forbears, the Treanors and the Clines of Milledgeville, had played essential roles in the establishment of this church. In fact, it is impossible to tell the history of Sacred Heart or Catholicism in Milledgeville without recounting something of the history of the Treanors and the Clines.

The first Mass in Milledgeville was celebrated in April 1845 by the Reverend J. J. O'Connell of the Order of St. Benedict in the rooms of the family of Hugh Donnelly Treanor, Flannery O'Connor's great-grandfather, in the

Newell Hotel (since demolished). O'Connor writes, "Mass was first said here in my great-grandfather's hotel room, later in his home on the piano." One of the most fascinating stories of O'Connor's ancestry on the maternal side is that Flannery's mother, Regina Cline (O'Connor), was the seventh of nine children of Margaret Ida Treanor, a daughter of Hugh Treanor, and widower Peter James Cline, who had already fathered seven children in his previous marriage to Kate Treanor, Margaret Ida's sister. O'Connor's great-grandfather Hugh Donnelly Treanor had moved in 1833 to Milledgeville from Locust Grove, Georgia, the state's first Catholic settlement. In 1848 he married Johannah Harty, Irish-born daughter of Patrick Harty from Tipperary, Ireland, among the first of O'Connor's ancestors to settle in this country.

The operator of a successful gristmill, Hugh Donnelly Treanor was the first Catholic resident of Milledgeville. Flannery's other great-grandfather on her mother's side, Peter Cline, had emigrated from Ireland in 1845 and was for a time a Latin teacher in Augusta, Georgia. Grandfather Peter James Cline was a successful businessman and prominent citizen in Milledgeville. He was elected the town's first Catholic mayor in 1888.

In 1850 the Roman Catholic Diocese of Savannah was established, Georgia having been, up to this point, a part of the Diocese of Charleston. In 1871 the editor of the *Union and Recorder*, Milledgeville's weekly newspaper, asserted the need for construction of a Catholic church, citing the useful contributions of Catholic citizens from abroad, but only in 1873 did Milledgeville Catholics meet and decide to build a church. Flannery O'Connor's grandfather, Peter Cline, presided at that meeting.

Later that year two property sales enabled the local Catholics to obtain the land on which Sacred Heart would be built. William McKinley sold forty feet of frontage property on Jefferson Street to William H. Gross, the bishop of Savannah. In September Mr. McKinley sold the corner lot at Hancock and N. Jefferson Streets to George Haas, who two days later sold the lot to Bishop Gross. Significantly, Mrs. Hugh Donnelly Treanor,

Sacred Heart Catholic Church, 1951. Photo by Robert W. Mann

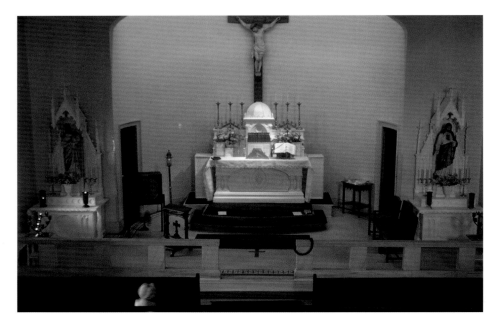

Flannery O'Connor's great-grandmother, bought the property for the church from Mr. Haas. On the cornerstone of the church building, a bronze plaque commemorates Mrs. Treanor's gift. Thus, for over a hundred years, the Treanor-Cline family has figured importantly in the life of Sacred Heart Church. (At her death at age ninety-nine in 1995, Regina Cline O'Connor left a significant financial bequest to Sacred Heart, an appropriate end to a life of generosity to the parish.)

Following an eloquent public address presented by Bishop Gross at the Statehouse in 1873, funds were soon raised for the building of the church on the site of the old LaFayette Hotel on the property described above. In 1874, as the church was nearing completion, an article in the *Union and Recorder* described the interior as "thirty by thirty feet with the ceiling twenty-one feet above the floor, curved at the angle of intersection with the walls, and a gallery across the end nine feet wide." The windows were

Gothic in style, containing handmade pressed glass that had previously been in the Lafayette Hotel. The sanctuary was designed to hold more than one hundred and fifty people. The steeple rose sixty feet in height. The total cost of construction, shocking by today's standards, was four thousand dollars.

After the completion of the structure in April 1874, the church was dedicated by Bishop Gross to the Sacred Heart of Jesus. In the early years of the church, priests from Macon, Augusta, and Savannah served the parish; the earliest resident pastor was the Reverend Robert Kennedy, who served from 1889 to 1904 and made improvements in the structure of the church, extending the building to allow for a larger sanctuary and sacristy. Another noteworthy priest serving the parish was the Reverend Richard Hamilton (1906–11), whose love of music and drama drew many young people to their first experience of the arts. Father Hamilton was presented with a seven-branched candelabrum for the sanctuary by the famous actress Sarah Bernhardt, a personal friend of the priest. That candelabrum continues in use today and is referred to simply as "the Sarah Bernhardt." The statue of the Virgin Mary would have been of particular importance to O'Connor, who, though certainly avoiding any sentimental statements of devotion to her, associated her, as poet Gerard Manley Hopkins did, with peaceful sleep: "Hopkins said she was the air we breathe, but I have come to realize her most in the gift of going to sleep. Life without her would be equivalent to me to life without sleep and as she contained Christ for a time, she seems to contain our life in sleep for a time so that we are able to wake up in peace."

In other landmark events in the history of the church, the first wedding in the new church united Peter James Cline and Kate Treanor on February 8, 1875. The first funeral from the church was that of Mary Treanor, the daughter of Hugh Treanor and Joanna Harty Treanor, April 10, 1876. Regina Cline and Edward Francis O'Connor were married at Sacred Heart on October 14, 1922. Funerals for both were conducted there as well.

Station of the Cross, present day

Following her family's move to Milledgeville in 1941, Flannery O'Connor knew the Reverend Joseph G. Cassidy and then the Reverend John D. Toomey; in fact, it was Father Cassidy who presided at her funeral in 1964. However, she would have certainly known earlier priests during the long and leisurely summer visits she made to her mother's home in Milledgeville prior to the family's permanent move there.

Membership in Sacred Heart at the time O'Connor attended church here in the 1950s and '60s was about fifty. Catholics were certainly a minority in Milledgeville, as they were in many parts of the South, but Sacred Heart continued to grow. In the early 1950s, Father Toomey began celebrating three weekend masses, and in September 1951 a Catholic school was opened for children from kindergarten through the sixth grade. The school was housed next door to the rectory and administered by the Sisters of St. Joseph. During the time that the Sisters of St. Joseph resided in Milledgeville, Flannery O'Connor briefly took piano lessons from Sister Loretta Costa of the order, although, according to O'Connor's own testimony, she possessed "the original tin ear," adding that "St. Cecilia wouldn't know what to do with me." Her attempts at playing the accordion earlier in her life "had nothing to do with music"; she said she liked the instrument because "it glittered and moved about." O'Connor's humor is often aimed at herself and is characterized by its comic exaggeration, and the subject of her musical insufficiency is no exception.

Unfortunately, the Catholic school was closed in 1956 because of the shortage of nuns in other areas of the country. Before and after the establishment of the Catholic school, the Sisters of Mercy came over from Macon each Sunday to teach Sunday School.

The most extensive renovation of the church occurred about nine years after Flannery O'Connor's death. In 1973, under the leadership of the Reverend Denis Dullea and at a cost of approximately fifty thousand dollars, gold carpeting was installed, gold velvet draperies were hung on the doors of each side of the altar and confessional, and a deep red-figured oriental runner was extended from the front door to the main altar. New chandeliers and pews were added, all the woodwork was restored to its natural finish, and the church was completely repainted. Sacred Heart celebrated its centennial in 1974, with a formal ceremony led by the arch-bishop of Atlanta, who blessed and rededicated the renovated church. In 1985 what was formerly the hall between the rectory and the church was renamed Flannery O'Connor Hall.

Today the membership of Sacred Heart is approximately three hundred and fifty. The increase was the result, to a large extent, of the influx of Cuban families to Milledgeville and Baldwin County following the Castro revolution in the early 1960s. Today there are four masses each weekend to accommodate the increased membership.

Flannery O'Connor's funeral, a low Requiem Mass, was held at 11:00 A.M. on Tuesday, August 4, at Sacred Heart Church, with Monsignor Joseph Cassidy officiating. The church was full, but not crowded. A number of trib-utes appeared in local and national newspapers, including the *New York Times*, which named O'Connor "one of the nation's most promising writers."

There are no Catholic church buildings in O'Connor's fiction. In fact, the only stories in which Catholicism plays an apparent role are "A Temple of the Holy Ghost," "The Displaced Person," and "The Enduring Chill." In the two last-named narratives, the priests, however bumbling in the former and stringent in the latter, are the catalysts of what we perceive to be the moments of grace for the smug, hard-souled protagonists. O'Connor does not wear her Catholicism on her sleeve in her fiction; she lived in the Bible Belt and was acutely aware of the perceptions of many Protestants of the Roman Catholic Church. She satirizes that ignorance and provincialism in her first novel *Wise Blood* and again in "The Displaced Person" when Mr. Shortley declares to his wife, "I ain't going to have the Pope of Rome tell me how to run no dairy."

There may be no Catholic church buildings in O'Connor's fiction, but Catholic belief underlies everything the author wrote. An unfaltering be-

"I measure God by everything I am not. I begin with that." (*Habit of Being*)

Entrance to Memory Hill
Cemetery

liever in the teaching authority and guidance of the Church, Flannery O'Connor asserted the need for humankind to submit to God with reverence, obedience, and discipline. As a Christian writer, O'Connor set herself the goal of "the accurate naming of the things of God." One's writerly prayer, she believed, should be to "ask God to let you see straight and write straight."

Memory Hill Cemetery

Flannery O'Connor was buried in the family plot in Memory Hill Cemetery on August 4, 1964. Visitors may locate the gravesite by turning left at the first paved road to the left of the main entrance to the cemetery and proceeding about half a city block to the Cline plot by the fence to the left of the road [East Side, Section A, Lot 39, Person 7]. The stone reads, "Mary Flannery O'Connor, daughter of Regina Lucille Cline and Edward Francis O'Connor, Jr., born in Savannah, Ga. March 25, 1925, died in Milledgeville, Ga. August 3, 1964." The body of Regina Cline O'Connor, who outlived her daughter by thirty-one years, lies between father and daughter. Other relatives are buried nearby.

On the South Square, set aside in 1804 for public use, the Methodist Church built a sanctuary in 1809 and established a church cemetery. The church eventually moved to Statehouse Square, the location of other churches, and South Square then became Milledgeville City Cemetery. In 1945 "Memory Hill" was added to the name of the Milledgeville City Cemetery, though today the area is commonly referred to simply as Memory Hill.

Listed on the National Register of Historic Places as part of the historic district of Milledgeville, Memory Hill contains a wide range of people from all walks of life, as well as many Georgia legislators. The statesman Carl Vinson is buried here, as well as Edwin F. Jemison, the young Confederate soldier whose image is among the most famous photographs of the Civil War; noted scientist Charles Herty; Dixie Haygood, also known as Annie Abbott, "the little Georgia Magnet," a spiritualist and magician; and Bill Miner, the "Grey Fox," one of the last outlaws of the American West. The unmarked graves of slaves can be found near the back of the cemetery, as can the graves of patients who once inhabited Central State Hospital.

Over the years the grave of Flannery O'Connor has become the objective of many a pilgrimage to Milledgeville and Memory Hill. Fans of O'Connor's work often leave flowers, coins, and other tokens on the gravesite, as well as poignant and appreciative letters to the deceased author, a strong testimony to the enduring power of her writing.

Gravestone of Mary Flannery O'Connor

Andalusia

THE PRIMARY LOCATION for the creation of Flannery O'Connor's major work, Andalusia is a beautiful, heavily forested farm located just inside the city limits of Milledgeville. At the time O'Connor lived here, from late 1950 to 1964, the farm was located well outside the city limits, "in the country." Now the 544-acre farm, though uncomfortably close to a rapidly developing commercial area, is a public trust and historic treasure, offering a restful haven to visitors, just as it offered its beauty and comfort to Flannery O'Connor years ago. This rural setting provided Flannery O'Connor with the fields and woods so important to her fiction, either as settings for central encounters, as in the purgatorial burning in "A Circle in the Fire" or the Christ-haunted forest in "A View of the Woods," or as significant background, suggesting the mystery of divine creation. Today the farm is open to visitors, who may walk the grounds and tour the house, as they gain understanding of Flannery O'Connor's work and her world.

Having graduated from Georgia State College for Women in 1945 and from the State University of Iowa Writers' Workshop in 1947, Flannery O'Connor did postgraduate work at Iowa and spent some time in New York, both at the Yaddo Foundation artists' retreat and in the city itself. However, because city life did not suit her, she became a boarder at the Ridgefield, Connecticut, home of Sally and Robert Fitzgerald, to whom she had been introduced by Robert Lowell in New York. This congenial

"Man, Gawd owns them woods and her too." ("A Circle in the Fire")

OPPOSITE: *Flannery O'Connor on crutches on the front steps of the Main House at Andalusia, 1962. Photo Joe McTyre* / Atlanta Constitution

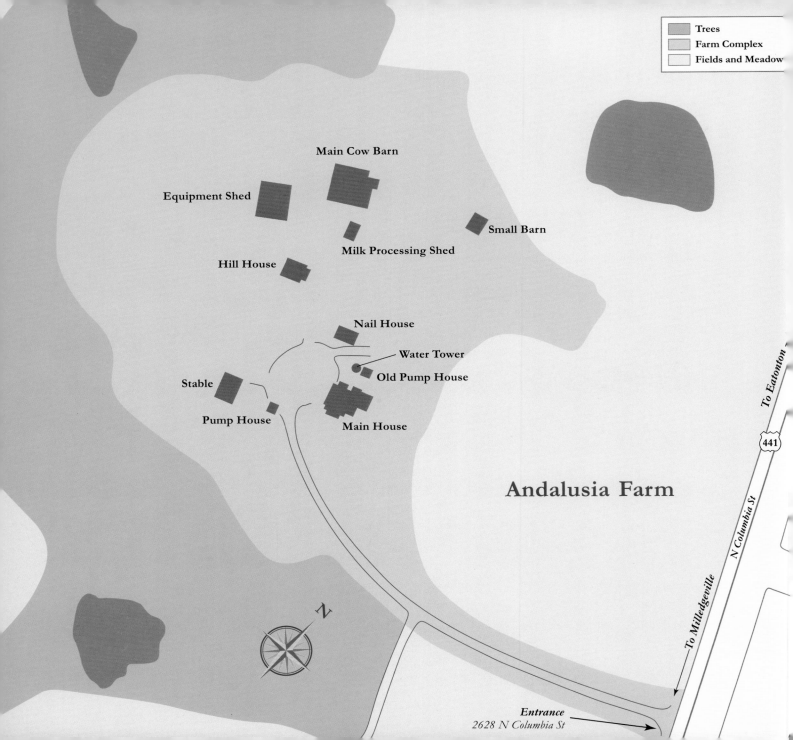

*Flannery O'Connor in the small
parlor at Andalusia, 1962. Photo Joe McTyre /
Atlanta Constitution*

arrangement was cut short when O'Connor became ill in late 1950 and was
forced to return to Milledgeville, where she was hospitalized and nearly
died. From 1951 until her death in 1964, O'Connor made her home at
Andalusia, which was more convenient for her than the Cline House in
town because she could enter the back door at ground level and because
her bedroom was on the first floor. Regina O'Connor also had a first-
floor bedroom, just behind Flannery's, and thus was able to supervise her
daughter's health, as well as the busy life of the farm.

After Flannery's death, Regina moved back into the Cline House, making daily visits to the farm to oversee its continuing activity. At the death of Regina O'Connor at age ninety-nine in 1995, the twenty-acre farm complex became the property of one of Regina's nieces, Margaret Florencourt Mann, and her husband, Robert. When Margaret died in 2002, Robert Mann took steps to establish Andalusia as a public trust, donating the farm to the Flannery O'Connor–Andalusia Foundation. In 2003 Regina's estate donated the remaining portion of Andalusia (with the exception of twenty-one acres belonging to Louise Florencourt, Margaret's sister) to the Foundation. Robert Mann died in 2006.

A Bit of Farm History

This farm and the land that it occupies have a long and rich history. There is evidence, for example, that those parts of Andalusia located above the flood plain were home to the Ocute tribe of Native Americans, first encountered by Hernando de Soto in 1540 when he crossed the Oconee River some six miles from where the city of Milledgeville would be established. These Native Americans left behind a wealth of pottery, tools, weapons, and, of course, place names. The abundance of wildlife, the fertile soil, and the comfortable climate would have been conducive to native habitation and to European settlement. Indeed, by the end of the eighteenth century, the Native Americans had ceded approximately three million acres between the Ogeechee and Oconee rivers.

Because agriculture was the basis of Georgia's economy in the nineteenth century, Baldwin County was home to many plantations; the land that we now know as Andalusia was part of one such plantation. Joseph Stovall was the earliest known occupant of this property, and in early title records the tract was named "the Stovall place." Stovall and his family lived in town, however, as was the custom of many planter farmers. The plantation consisted of a total of seventeen hundred acres along Tobler Creek, just four miles north of Milledgeville. At the death of Stovall, the tract was purchased by Nathan Hawkins, who was mayor of Milledgeville in the 1850s and represented Baldwin County in the state legislature. Like Stovall, Hawkins lived in town, although he built the farmhouse and became one of the most prosperous plantation owners in the area; he owned at one time more than one hundred slaves. When General Sherman invaded Baldwin County in 1864, Hawkins's home was spared, but the plantation was stripped. The slaves were, of course, later freed, causing the Hawkins family great financial hardship. With Hawkins's death in 1870, 1,134 acres of the plantation were auctioned and awarded to Colonel Thomas Johnson of Kentucky as the result of a judgment in a lawsuit against Hawkins. The remaining tract, encompassing the house and outbuildings, was subject to the life estate of Nathan Hawkins's widow, Amanda. Visitors will be interested to know that this tract, the exact size of which was in dispute in real estate documents for the next thirty-five years, today constitutes the boundaries of Andalusia.

Johnson, a well-respected businessman and farmer, maintained his interest in the Hawkins Plantation for thirty years, though he never lived there. In 1905 he sold the property to Madison McCraw of Milledgeville, who then sold half of his acreage to Milledgeville judge John T. Allen. When the descendants of Amanda Hawkins would not recognize that the property automatically reverted to the Johnson estate at her death, a court battle ensued, with the tract awarded to the Johnson estate.

Madison McCraw's widow and his two daughters inherited the property at his death in 1916. With the paving of the Old Sheffield Wagon Road, also known as Clines Bridge Wagon Road (now U.S. 441), the property was split on a north-south angle, with approximately 712 acres on the west and fewer than one thousand on the east. When Mrs. McCraw died intestate in 1930, Hugh T. Cline, brother of Regina Cline O'Connor, was appointed her estate administrator. Most of the land on the east side of the road was acquired by Judge Allen's estate, and that on the west by Mrs. McCraw's estate. The latter was subdivided into three lots, with lots 1 and 2 matching almost exactly the current boundaries of Andalusia.

The Cline family first acquired the farm in 1931, when Dr. Bernard McHugh Cline, brother of Hugh T. Cline and Regina Cline O'Connor, purchased the 325-acre tract; the purchase was completed by 1933, at which time Virginia McCraw, one of the McCraw daughters, sold her 225-acre tract (Lot 2) to Bernard Cline. An eye-ear-nose-throat specialist practicing in Atlanta, Bernard Cline came to Milledgeville only on weekends, though he continued to purchase wooded tracts to the north of the farm. With the help of employees and family members like Frank Florencourt, husband of Regina Cline O'Connor's sister Agnes, the farm became fully functional. In the early 1940s Bernard Cline sent Regina O'Connor to Atlanta to train as a bookkeeper for the dairy he intended to establish at the farm. The growing success of the farm paralleled that of the surrounding community: Milledgeville and Baldwin County were continuing to show signs of progress during this time, with airport and bus transportation, the installation of natural gas lines, and radio broadcasting.

With the sudden death of Dr. Bernard Cline in January of 1947, the farm was left as a life estate to Regina O'Connor and another brother, Louis Cline, who worked out of Atlanta as a sales representative for King Hardware. (Bernard also left some tracts north of the farm to various family members, but this acreage had never been part of the original farm.) The life estate of the farm itself was later converted to full ownership, with Regina O'Connor and Louis Cline as co-owners until Louis's death in 1973. The two siblings expanded the dairy with two hundred acres of pasture, several hay fields and livestock ponds, keeping the rest of the property in woodlands for selective timbering. Because Louis Cline kept his job in Atlanta and came to Milledgeville for the most part only on weekends, Regina O'Connor assumed primary responsibility for the farm, managing it with tenants and hired help. Mrs. O'Connor's success as a widow managing a farm drew much attention in the 1950s, as might be expected.

Bernard Cline had named the property Sorrel Farm because of the sorrel horses he kept there. However, when Flannery O'Connor met a descendant of one of the previous owners, who told her that the farm was originally called Andalusia (ostensibly after the province in southern Spain), the farm was renamed Andalusia. So it has been called since 1947. Today the association of the name Andalusia with Flannery O'Connor is a strong one; most of her finest writing was, in fact, produced at the farm, though O'Connor was always quick to assert that she *farmed* "only from the rocking chair."

The Main House

The primary dwelling at Andalusia, built about 1850, is a plantation plain-style farmhouse (two-over-two, as it is sometimes called) with conventional white clapboard exterior. Flannery O'Connor and her mother took up residence here, for all intents and purposes abandoning the Cline House on Greene Street, when O'Connor experienced her serious initial bout with lupus in December of 1950. With the onset of the disease, O'Connor returned home from Ridgefield, Connecticut, where she had boarded with Sally and Robert Fitzgerald and their growing family and where she had continued to work on her first novel, *Wise Blood*. The return to Milledgeville was to be permanent, and Andalusia farm became O'Connor's locus of reality. Although the circumstances of her return to Andalusia and Milledgeville were certainly lamentable, most students of O'Connor's writing believe that the return to her Georgia roots was indeed serendipitous for her fiction. With the exception of some traveling when she was able, O'Connor lived the last and most productive years of her life in Milledgeville. The isolation and quiet of life on the farm, per-

haps quite surprisingly, suited O'Connor, who found comfort and inspiration, often comedic, in the quotidian. In fact, in her letters at least, she rather enjoyed the image of herself as a quiet-living, provincial woman, claiming, "There won't be any biographies of me because, for only one reason, lives spent between the house and the chicken yard do not make exciting copy."

The steep front steps to the screened porch of the Main House were, as one might expect, an obstacle to Flannery O'Connor after she became ill; at least one famous photograph, however, shows O'Connor on her crutches standing at the top of those steps. She was able to enter the house by ascending only a few steps through the back door, and she and Regina lived essentially on the first floor of the house. The wide front porch with its opaque screens provided Flannery and Regina with ample visiting space for social occasions and a comfortable place for relaxation, especially in the spring and fall. The rocking chairs that now grace the porch were given in honor of those special friends who were often guests of the O'Connors and enjoyed porch time at Andalusia.

As visitors enter the house, they may immediately view Flannery's bedroom, the first room on the left. Here, in this plain and rather austere setting, O'Connor created many of her most memorable characters and plots. The simple single bed, with its tall wooden headboard, is covered by the same plain spread that O'Connor used. The Morris chair and chiffonier were also part of the furnishings in O'Connor's day. However, the desk and typewriter are not those used by O'Connor; her actual desk, with its simple, makeshift orange-crate shelving, and her manual typewriter are part of the O'Connor Collection at Georgia College & State University. (The typewriter in the bedroom at Andalusia probably belonged to Regina O'Connor.) When she wrote, O'Connor never faced a window; that vista would have been too distracting. As her letters and lectures attest, O'Connor was a disciplined writer, sitting before the typewriter every day, never waiting for the

OPPOSITE: *The Main House, present day*

inconstant muse to strike. As though in witness to that discipline and to the difficulties illness made in the fulfillment of O'Connor's vocation, the metal crutches are propped near the desk. She was forced to rely on them when the medication for her disease caused her bones to deteriorate.

The record player on the west wall of the room was given to O'Connor by the sisters at Our Lady of Perpetual Care in Atlanta. The painting of Andalusia's resident farmer Louise Hill over the bookcases that contained many of O'Connor's own collection of books (including theology, philosophy, fiction, and poetry) was painted by Robert Hood of Florida, a friend and the husband of another lupus sufferer, Dean Hood; the Hoods visited O'Connor at Andalusia and made her a gift of the painting. O'Connor reciprocated by presenting the Hoods with her painting of the male choir, which was donated at Dean Hood's death to the O'Connor Collection at GCSU, where it may be viewed. The door in the rear of the room leads to what was the bedroom of Regina O'Connor, whose presence nearby was essential to O'Connor in much of her illness. Regina's bedroom has been converted into an office for the executive director of the Flannery O'Connor–Andalusia Foundation.

Across the hall from Flannery's bedroom, the dining room contains the O'Connors' oak table, Victorian chairs with cane bottoms, a marble-top sideboard, a marble-top chest, and a spool-turned étagère. Regina O'Connor, quite a seamstress, made the curtains here and in Flannery's bedroom. She also made many of Flannery's clothes.

Regina's office was located where the gift shop is now located. From here Regina managed the dairy farm and the workers. The upright piano on the back right wall of the gift shop was a family heirloom. The sink in the front right corner of the shop was a common feature in nineteenth-century houses; in fact, there are sinks in each of the upstairs bedrooms. The Flemish-style painting on the left back wall is of unknown origin but was a part of the O'Connor décor.

"I'm a full-time believer in writing habits, pedestrian as it all may sound. You may be able to do without them if you have genius but most of us only have talent and this is simply something that has to be assisted all the time by physical and mental habits or it dries up and blows away. I see it happen all the time. Of course you have to make your habit in this conform to what you *can* do. I write only about two hours every day because that's all the energy I have, but I don't let anything interfere with those two hours, at the same time and the same place. This doesn't mean I produce much out of the two hours. Sometimes I work for months and have to throw everything away, but I don't think any of that was time wasted. Something goes on that makes it easier when it does come well. And the fact is if you don't sit there every day, the day it would come well, you won't be sitting there." (*The Habit of Being*)

OPPOSITE: *The front porch of the Main House, present day*

The entry hall

Flannery O'Connor's bedroom, with her crutches and one of her typewriters

The mantle in Flannery O'Connor's bedroom

The kitchen table where
Flannery and Regina O'Connor
took many of their meals

The family dining room

The back (guest) bedroom in the Main House

The kitchen, just off the gift shop to the right, contains the actual appliances and furniture that the O'Connors used, except that the positioning of many of the pieces is different from that of O'Connor's time. Regina and Flannery took most of their meals at the square, sturdy kitchen table. Beyond the kitchen is a small sitting room and additional bedroom added by Louis Cline in 1959. The sitting room, with its large windows affording bright light and its comfortable ambience, housed additional books in Flannery's collection, in two massive bookcases that sat between the south windows. Those bookcases were donated by Regina O'Connor to

Georgia College & State University and may now be seen in the O'Connor Collection there.

The upstairs of the house contains two identical guest bedrooms with one bath between. Only one of the bedrooms is now open for viewing. Those who have seen the Glenn Jordan production of *The Displaced Person* may recall a number of interior shots of Andalusia, including Mrs. McIntyre's anguished reaction to Mr. Guizac's attempt to save his cousin from the gas chamber by marrying her to one of Mrs. McIntyre's African American workers. The farm's outbuildings also figure in that film, which was shot almost entirely on location at Andalusia.

Who can view the barn behind the house without thinking that Joy/Hulga Hopewell may still be lurking, without her wooden leg, in its loft? This building in O'Connor's day, of course, was part of a working dairy farm, as were the other outbuildings, in various states of disrepair today. The home of Jack and Louise Hill was somewhat larger than the usual tenant houses of the day. Its proximity to the Main House enabled Jack and Louise to be available when Regina needed them, although their antics and their fractiousness were sometimes a little too close for comfort, as Flannery's letters indicate. Nevertheless, O'Connor's fine ear for dialect and southern speech patterns in general undoubtedly benefited from such proximity.

O'Connor and the Land

Flannery O'Connor's use of the land is not like that of William Faulkner, for whom the South's complicated and tragic history is inextricably tied to the envy and greed of the propertyless for property, for land, with all the bizarre comedy and violence entailed by that age-old conflict. To be sure, O'Connor saw humanity as fallen and always subject to envy and greed, among other sins; her vision, however, belongs to Christian proph-

"[T]he toast-colored hat disappeared down the hole and the girl was left, sitting on the straw in the dusty sunlight." ("Good Country People")

OPPOSITE: *Flannery O'Connor sitting in front of her private library in the small parlor, 1962. Photo Joe McTyre* / Atlanta Constitution

The back of the Main House, 1951.
Photo by Robert W. Mann

OPPOSITE: *Driveway and gate into Andalusia, Highway 441 North, present day*

The milk-processing shed, present day

ecy, wherein the rural landscape, with its inevitable long line of trees, serves as the setting, at times almost ritualistic, for the individual's confrontation with evil and with the possibility of God's redemptive grace. O'Connor, unlike Faulkner, is not concerned with the actual history of the South or with any kind of collective white guilt; her fiction is centered on the individual search for salvation. Thus, even stories like "A Late Encounter with the Enemy," the only one of O'Connor's works to be even tangentially concerned with the Civil War and thus with southern history, is essentially concerned with the uselessness of a life that in its own pride and narcissism can find no meaning in history.

In O'Connor's presentation of farm life in such stories as "A Circle in the Fire," "Greenleaf," and "A View of the Woods," the natural world is

"The fortress line of trees was a hard granite blue, the wind had risen overnight and the sun had come up a pale gold." ("A Circle in the Fire")

"The trees were full of silver-white sunlight and the meanest of them sparkled." ("A Good Man Is Hard to Find")

The old well pump, present day

sacramental: as the narratives progress, open spaces and woods assume increasingly significant, if not symbolic, resonance. In "A Circle in the Fire," O'Connor writes, "The fortress line of trees was a hard granite blue, the wind had risen overnight and the sun had come up a pale gold." Similarly, this description of pastureland in "The River" could well have derived from O'Connor's own dairy farm setting: "At the bottom of the hill, the woods opened suddenly onto a pasture dotted here and there with black and white cows and sloping down, tier after tier, to a broad orange stream where the reflection of the sun was set like a diamond."

Frequently in O'Connor's work the reader encounters dramatic images of the sun, centrally placed to emphasize O'Connor's sacramental view of nature and the centuries-old play of "sun" with "son," to suggest the central event of human history, in O'Connor's view: the sacrifice of Christ, the Son of God, and His resurrection. In fact, in "A Good Man Is Hard to Find," the sun illuminates and gives life to all, as suggested by "The trees were full of silver-white sunlight and the meanest of them sparkled." One can only surmise that the view from the wide front porch at Andalusia, or from any vista on the grounds, provided O'Connor with the images of the sacred spaces around which many of her finest stories would cohere. For this deeply spiritual writer, as for the British poet Gerard Manley Hopkins whom O'Connor much admired, the world is "charged" with the majesty of God, a fact that is clearly evident in the natural world.

In addition to providing O'Connor with the profound beauty of the natural world through the rhythms of the seasons, life on the farm presented her with many down-to-earth and comic moments as well. As the letters in *The Habit of Being* attest, O'Connor reveled in the antics of the tenants Jack and Louise Hill, who had a propensity for quarreling when under the influence of alcohol. The Hill House, to the left of and

"He saw it, in his hallucination, as if someone were wounded behind the woods and the trees were bathed in blood." ("A View of the Woods")

"She stared at the violent black streak bounding toward her as if she had no sense of distance, as if she could not decide at once what his intention was, and the bull had buried his head in her lap, like a wild tormented lover, before her expression changed." ("Greenleaf")

"In the deepening light everything was taking on a mysterious hue. The pasture was growing a peculiar glassy green and the streak of highway had turned lavender. She braced herself for a final assault and this time her voice rolled out over the pasture. 'Go on,' she yelled, 'call me a hog! Call me a hog again. From hell. Call me a wart hog from hell. Put that bottom rail on top. There'll still be a top and bottom!'" ("Revelation")

The home of Jack and Louise Hill, 1951 (photo by Robert W. Mann) and present day

behind the Main House at Andalusia, was the scene of many such dramatic episodes, which, while exasperating to Regina O'Connor, afforded her daughter occasional amusement. Louise, especially, was known for her outspokenness and humorous flair; she remained at Andalusia for some years after O'Connor's death in 1964 and always greeted visitors to the farm with warmth and genuine respect for the achievement of "Miss Flannery."

Regina O'Connor herself possessed a strong personality, and her dealings with farmhands and the locals also provided her daughter with material. Most readers of O'Connor's fiction notice the author's frequent use of single (widowed or divorced) female farm owners as central figures, as in "Good Country People," "The Displaced Person," "A Temple of the Holy Ghost," and "The Enduring Chill." While these stories are most certainly fiction and thus employ imaginative re-creation of life at the farm, there is no doubt that Flannery O'Connor made use of the life she knew upon her return to Milledgeville.

O'Connor's fine essay "The King of the Birds," describing her intense interest in and ultimate obsession with peafowl, contains several of her most comic and revealing anecdotes, all set on the farm and based on her experience with the more than fifty peacocks she at one time owned. Regina O'Connor, initially filled with misgivings about the peacock enterprise, provides some of the comedy in this essay, as the peacock tribe grows and wreaks havoc with her flowerbeds. In Flannery's account, Regina decides to erect hundreds of yards of twenty-four-inch-high fence to protect these beds, contending that the peacocks don't have enough sense to jump over a low fence: "'If it were a high wire,'" Regina argues, "'they would jump onto it and over, but they don't have sense enough to jump over a low wire.'"

One day when a country family with its many children tumble out of their car and behold the peacock with its glorious tail unfurled, one of the children asks, "Whut is thet thang?" To which the old grandfather replies,

"Her mother let the conversation drop and the child's round face was lost in thought. She turned it toward the window and looked out over a stretch of pasture land that rose and fell with a gathering greenness until it touched the dark woods. The sun was a huge red ball like an elevated Host drenched in blood and when it sank out of sight, it left a line in the sky like a red clay road hanging over the trees." ("A Temple of the Holy Ghost")

OPPOSITE: *Flossie, the hinny who belonged to Regina O'Connor, still lives at Andalusia.*

politely removing his hat, "Churren . . . that's the king of the birds!" On another day, an old black woman, upon seeing the peacock, mutters, "Amen! Amen!" O'Connor concludes, "I have tried imagining that the single peacock I see before me is the only one I have, but then one comes to join him; another flies off the roof, four or five crash out of the crepe-myrtle hedge; from the pond one screams and from the barn I hear the dairyman denouncing another that has got into the cow-feed. My kin are given to such phrases as 'Let's face it.'"

In O'Connor's fiction, an individual's response to the peacock seems indicative of his or her understanding of God's presence, as is clearly evident in her story "The Displaced Person," in which the peacock figures strongly. In addition to its powerful suggestions of the peacock's symbolic importance, O'Connor's "The King of the Birds," originally published in *Holiday* magazine, contains much peacock lore, including practical information about the bird and his habits, a fact that might be surprising to readers who think the writer had no practical side. For some years after O'Connor's death, peacocks remained on the farm until the number fell to one. He was last seen enjoying a view of the woods, for O'Connor believed that, in the end, the peacock would have the last word.

"The priest let his eyes wander toward the birds. They had reached the middle of the lawn. The cock stopped suddenly and curving his neck backwards, he raised his tail and spread it with a shimmering timbrous noise. Tiers of small pregnant suns floated in a green-gold haze over his head. The priest stood transfixed, his jaw slack. Mrs. McIntyre wondered where she had ever seen such an idiotic old man. 'Christ will come like that!' he said in a loud gay voice and wiped his hand over his mouth and stood there, gaping."
("The Displaced Person")

OPPOSITE: *Flannery O'Connor is often associated with the numerous peacocks that used to roam the grounds at Andalusia.*

The Monastery of the Holy Spirit

PERHAPS ONE OF THE GREATEST GIFTS that Flannery O'Connor received after her return to Milledgeville was the friendship she enjoyed with several of the Trappist monks at Our Lady of Holy Spirit Abbey, now the Monastery of the Holy Spirit, at 2625 Georgia Highway 212 sw near Conyers, about 55 miles from Milledgeville and about 45 miles from Atlanta.

The Georgia monastery (called an abbey because it is presided over by an abbot) was established in 1944 by the Cistercians of Our Lady of Gethsemane Monastery, located outside Louisville, Kentucky. The Trappists are a part of the Cistercian Order of the Strict Observance, though not all Cistercians are Trappists. As its full name suggests, the Cistercian Order is the strictest of the Roman Catholic Church. Following the decree of St. Benedict, who espoused "ora et labora," prayer and work, the Cistercians have been devoted to the contemplative life in community since the twelfth century. The monastery at Gethsemane was established in 1849, some one hundred years before the one at Conyers.

Most famous among American Trappists was Thomas Merton, known as Father Louis, whose spiritual memoir *The Seven Storey Mountain*, published in 1948, recounts his early restlessness, loneliness, and profligate youth; his later conversion to Catholicism; and his entry into the Cistercian Order. Merton's book was greatly influential on an entire generation of spiritual seekers and continues to be so today. Although Flannery

OPPOSITE: *One of the founding monks of Our Lady of Holy Spirit Abbey. The monastery, established in 1944, was situated in this large barn until the cloister was built. Courtesy, Georgia Archives, Vanishing Georgia Collection, roc021*

O'Connor and the Trappist Thomas Merton never met, each clearly respected the other. On Merton's part, indeed, the feeling was profound; at O'Connor's death, he wrote in the Catholic magazine *Jubilee*, "When I read Flannery O'Connor, I do not think of Hemingway, or Katherine Anne Porter, or Sartre, but rather of someone like Sophocles. What more can you say for a writer? I write her name with honor, for all the truth and all the craft with which she shows man's fall and his dishonor."

Many young men in the 1940s were so inspired by *The Seven Storey Mountain* that Gethsemane Abbey was virtually overrun with aspirants, to the point that tents were raised in the cloister courtyard to house them. The problem with overcrowding, a happy one indeed for the Cistercians, led to the founding of a "daughter house" in the forests of central Georgia. In March of 1944 some twenty monks left Gethsemane for what was Honey Creek Plantation, a cotton farm of fourteen hundred acres in Rockdale County, just thirty miles east of Atlanta in an area that was then completely undeveloped. For eight months the monks lived in the hayloft of a barn also housing cows and chickens, while they built the initial monastery from unseasoned pine timber. This building, the monks' first real home in Georgia, came to be known as the Pineboard Monastery.

The monks then began work on the twelve-year project that resulted in the permanent monastery, built under the guidance of an architect, a supervisor, and a carpenter. Even though the initial plans called for a brick edifice, funds were lacking, and the monks had to resort to concrete, which they mixed and poured themselves. The lovely chapel with its high stained glass windows and simple rose window featuring Our Lady is appropriately austere for an order devoted to prayer and contemplation and bound by a vow of silence. After all, the monks have retreated from the noisy, distracting secular world in order to give God and His Word their undivided attention. At the time of the profession of his vocation, the Cistercian makes three promises, according to the Rule of St. Benedict: obedience, stability, and conversion of manners. The monk must be obedient to his superiors,

lead a balanced life of work and prayer within community, and practice poverty and chastity. The life of prayer, both in solitude and in community, is central to the monk's life. The choir stalls on either side of the chapel provide the gathering place for the monks' communal prayer life, which begins with matins at four in the morning and continues through vespers and compline in the evening.

Although silence is not enforced at Holy Spirit Abbey, it is desired, even in the performance of simple, everyday chores. A healthy balance of prayer, contemplation, and work is the aim of the Cistercians. In order to be self-sustaining, the monks have in the past managed a dairy herd and beef cattle, as well as a hay business and a stained-glass shop. Today the monastery operates a gift shop, which features religious artifacts, note cards and stationery, homemade bread, and condiments. The bonsai collection, famous throughout the Southeast, is also available to visitors, who may seek advice about the plants or make purchases. The guest house is open throughout the year for retreatants of both sexes and all denominations and religious affiliation. The abbey sponsors special weekend retreats on subjects of topical interest such as "The Trinity and Science" and "Spirituality for Judges and Lawyers," as well as on more traditional topics, such as prayer and vocation discernment.

Flannery O'Connor made her initial visit to Holy Spirit Abbey in 1959, when, in a letter of May 30 she describes "finally" getting there and meeting Father Paul Bourne, who was to become one of her good friends. After that first visit, O'Connor wrote that she intended to give the abbey some peacocks, an intention that she fulfilled some time later. O'Connor's peacocks remained at the abbey for about fifteen years, until their noise was deemed too disturbing for the monks' good. The peacocks were then sent to Ohio to live but were later killed by a fox. Stories about "Flannery's peacocks" continue to be told at the abbey to this day. The peacocks have been succeeded by some very fierce geese at the lake beside the abbey; they are often fed by the monastery's more courageous guests.

O'Connor understood the common stereotypes of monkish life. As early as the writing of *Wise Blood*, she has Mrs. Flood, the baffled landlady of Hazel Motes, reproach Hazel for wearing barbed wire and walking on glass. Mrs. Flood thinks that he "might as well be one of those monks. . . . He might as well be in a monkery." In a later story "The Life You Save May Be Your Own," O'Connor allows the con man Tom T. Shiftlet this powerful line: "The monks of old slept in their coffins." Oddly enough, Shiftlet is

Stained glass window behind the altar

drawing a parallel between this monastic practice and his own decision to sleep in the car that he hopes to acquire in a trade with Mrs. Crater for her daughter and "a man around the house." To his remark about the monks, Mrs. Crater responds, "But they wasn't as advanced as we are." Playing on the false measures defining progress in the modern world, O'Connor scathingly attacks the ignorance and provincialism of the Mrs. Craters among us, who have no understanding of the ascetic tradition, which has long involved the recognition of our common mortality—*memento mori* ("Remember you must die"). That, of course, is not all that Lucynell Crater, "ravenous for a son-in-law," does not understand.

Clearly O'Connor came to admire and respect Father Paul, a warm, intelligent, and well-read man and, to Regina O'Connor's delight, an accomplished gardener. In fact, Father Paul as a master gardener over-saw the bonsai nursery for years and was often sought out by other bonsai enthusiasts. Although leaving the monastery was rarely possible for the monks, Father Paul and the abbot at the time, Dom Augustine Moore, paid Flannery and Regina a visit in the spring of 1960 to try to persuade Flannery to become involved in a project involving Our Lady of Perpetual Help Cancer Home in Atlanta. Flannery had previously been approached by the nuns there to write the story of a child at the home who had a terrible cancer that grew out of one side of her face and who had recently died. The nuns considered little Mary Ann a saint and believed that her story should be told. Although O'Connor declined to write the story, she found the facts compelling: "What interests me in it is simply the mystery, the agony that is given in strange ways to children." Finally persuading the nuns to write the story themselves, O'Connor agreed to review the manuscript, which she then attempt-ed to free of its "obnoxious pieties," an apparently difficult chore in-deed. She reported to her publisher Robert Giroux that Father Paul was amused that she was asked to do this; according to O'Connor, he "asked

The grave of Flannery's friend Father Paul Bourne is located behind the church.

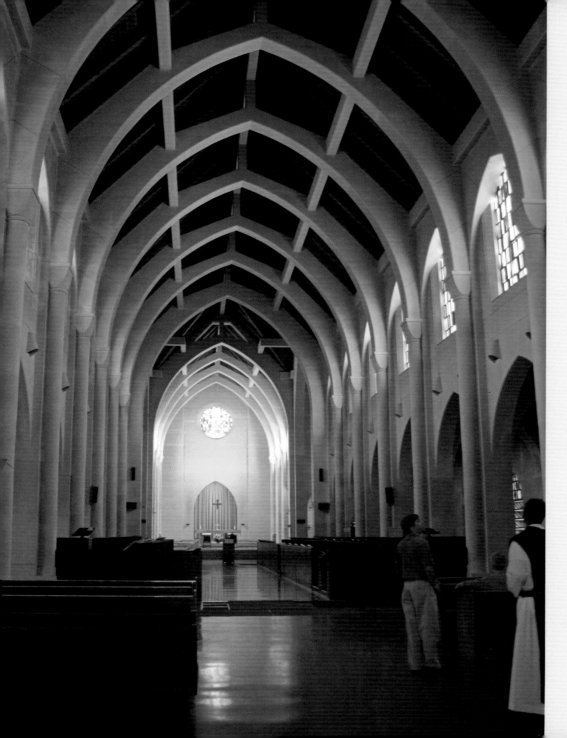

Nave of the monastery's church

[the nuns] which of my murder stories gave them the idea I should help them with it."

O'Connor had agreed to write "a little introduction" to the nuns' account, and so she did, though that piece of writing is anything but small. In the opinion of many O'Connor scholars, this essay, serving as the introduction to *A Memoir of Mary Ann*, is one of the finest nonfiction pieces that O'Connor ever wrote; it is certainly the most revelatory of her tough-minded faith and of her response to secular humanism. The essay is essential reading for those who want to understand O'Connor's work and, for that matter, the writer herself.

O'Connor's first visit to the church at the monastery occurred in November of 1961, about a year after its completion. She described the sanctuary as "unbelievable," and one can only infer that a great part of her awe had to do with the monks' dedication and skill, for they had built the church essentially with their own hands. Her friendship with Father Paul and Dom Augustine continued with visits back and forth until O'Connor's death in 1964. Both Father Paul and Dom Augustine died in the 1990s; they are buried in the monastery cemetery behind the church.

Although Flannery O'Connor had great respect for the monastic tradition, she herself never felt any call to such a vocation. She was consistently self-deprecating in discussing her abilities at contemplation and even prayer: "I am no good at meditating. This doesn't mean that I get right on with contemplating. I don't do either. If I attempt to keep my mind on the mysteries of the rosary, I am soon thinking about something else, entirely non-religious in nature." Of course, O'Connor always sought to avoid anything approaching public displays of piety or sentimentality, and she thus inevitably plays down her own spiritual practices. To be sure, however, Flannery O'Connor's gift was of another sort. She believed that her talent as a writer was a gift from God and therefore a grace and responsibility that she took very seriously until her dying day.

"One of the tendencies of our age is to use the suffering of children to discredit the goodness of God, and once you have discredited His goodness, you are done with Him. . . . Ivan Karamazov cannot believe, as long as one child is in torment; Camus' hero cannot accept the divinity of Christ, because of the massacre of the innocents. In this popular pity, we mark our gain in sensibility and our loss in vision. If other ages felt less, they saw more, even though they saw with the blind, prophetical, unsentimental eye of acceptance, which is to say, of faith. In the absence of this faith now, we govern by tenderness. It is a tenderness which, long since cut off from the person of Christ, is wrapped in theory. When tenderness is detached from the source of tenderness, its logical outcome is terror. It ends in forced labor camps and in the fumes of the gas chamber." ("Introduction," *A Memoir of Mary Ann*)

St. John the Baptist
Cathedral on
Lafayette Square

Catholicism in Georgia

BEFORE THE REVOLUTIONARY WAR, Catholics had not been accepted in Georgia. However, the devotion of Polish count Casimir Pulaski to the cause of Savannah greatly aided Catholic acceptance. The Catholic nobleman's valiant service and the courage and dedication of Savannah's Irish Catholics in the Seige of Savannah underscored the revolutionary emphasis on individual liberty and freedom of religion and gained for Catholics some rights in the state constitution of 1777. Nonetheless, they were still unable to hold political office. Only with the formal acceptance of the United States Constitution in 1789 did Catholics achieve equal rights under Georgia law. Equal rights did not assure assimilation or even understanding, however; Catholics in Georgia would continue to struggle for acceptance well into the twentieth century, a fact of which Flannery O'Connor was well aware.

Various English and European Catholics settled in Georgia in the late eighteenth century. In the early 1790s, for example, a group of English Catholics left the economic hardship of Maryland and settled in an area near Locust Grove, Georgia, south of what is now the city of Atlanta. The Fitzgeralds, ancestors of the family of Margaret Mitchell's mother, were among those Catholics. They were soon joined in that settlement by Catholics from Tipperary, Ireland, ancestors, on both sides, of Flannery O'Connor's family. Also in the late eighteenth century French Catholics settled in Savannah, and other Catholic communities were established in

Augusta and on the coast. However, because initially the Vatican assigned no priests to Georgia, early Catholic communities strove simply to survive. Although the Savannah Catholic community eventually brought two French priests to the state, the distance between Catholic communities in Georgia and the rest of the South was problematic.

Realizing this problem, the Vatican in 1820 created the Diocese of Charleston, which was to cover North Carolina and South Carolina as well as Georgia. The priest chosen to head this diocese was John England, a thirty-four-year-old Irishman who, for more than twenty years, served the diocese, recruiting priests and creating an order of nuns, the Sisters of Mercy, who came to Georgia in the 1840s. The Sisters of Mercy settled across Georgia, from Savannah to Macon, Athens, and Atlanta. Their devotion to education and health care led them to teach and operate schools and hospitals throughout the state. Bishop England made his greatest headway, however, in establishing more congenial relations with southern Protestants. He admired American religious freedom and made friends with Protestants; more importantly for the acceptance of Catholics in the South, the bishop, though he did not sanction slavery, condemned those outsiders who criticized the institution. Thus he won the support and trust of many southern leaders. In reality, of course, the position of the Roman Catholic Church on slavery was as equivocal as that of its Protestant counterpart.

By 1850 there were more than five thousand Catholics in Georgia, causing the Vatican to create the Diocese of Savannah, which would remain the center of Catholicism in Georgia into the early twentieth century. Many German and Irish Catholics settled in Savannah by the middle of the nineteenth century, among whom were Flannery O'Connor's Irish forbears.

Just before the Civil War, the Diocese of Savannah was served by its third bishop, the French-born Augustin Verot who—as though the embodiment of the fears of the early English Protestants in Georgia—came from St. Augustine, Florida, where he had served for many years. Verot was a fierce supporter of the Confederacy; he had defended slavery as early

Monk in prayer at Our Lady of Holy Spirit Abbey in Conyers

as 1861 in a sermon in Florida, causing him to be nicknamed the "Rebel Bishop." As a number of commentators have noted, Catholic loyalty to the Confederacy, if not directly to the cause of slavery, enabled Catholics to be more easily assimilated into Georgia life. After all, Catholic men served in the Confederate army, Catholic priests were often the only ministers at the infamous prison camp at Andersonville, and the Sisters of Mercy ministered in Confederate hospitals. Furthermore, the Sisters of Mercy continued to take care of the family of President Jefferson Davis after the defeat of the Confederacy. The so-called poet-priest of the Confederacy, the Reverend Abram Ryan, edited *Banner of the South*, a pro-South newspaper, from Augusta after the war.

During General William Tecumseh Sherman's siege of Atlanta on his march to the sea, Atlanta priest Thomas O'Reilly persuaded Sherman not to burn the Shrine of the Immaculate Conception, as well as St. Philip's Episcopal Cathedral, Central Presbyterian Church, and other Protestant churches in the city. Indeed, according to legend, when General Sherman reached Savannah on December 22, 1864, he was so overwhelmed by the city's beauty that he sent a telegram to President Lincoln offering him the city as a Christmas present. One might therefore argue that what Catholics loyal to the southern cause could not do, the beauty of the region was able to accomplish.

One of the consequences of Catholic loyalty to the Confederacy was the joining of Catholic primary schools to the local school systems, an arrangement that continued until the early twentieth century. Among many non-Catholic Georgians from this time on, acceptance of Roman Catholicism grew. When Savannah's Cathedral of St. John the Baptist burned in 1898, many non-Catholics assisted in raising the funds to build the new church. This edifice remains today one of Savannah's greatest achievements, one in which all Savannahians take pride.

For many Georgians, however, accepting Catholics was very difficult, and anti-Catholicism festered in the early decades of the twentieth century. Some Georgians began to feel threatened by the sheer growth of the Catholic Church, especially the addition of Italian, Lebanese, Hungarian, and African American Catholics to the predominantly Irish Catholic community and the assignment of foreign priests to Georgia parishes. Both sides on occasion employed tactics of desperation. In the 1890s Patrick Walsh of Augusta, Georgia's best-known Catholic politician, who edited the *Augusta Chronicle* and served in the legislature for years, met the challenge of Tom Watson of the Populist Party through shameful means, including stuffing ballot boxes in some areas. Walsh went on to become mayor of Augusta and the leading Catholic in Georgia politics, but his power and certain of his tactics were not the reassurance some fearful Georgia Protestants needed. Thus at the same time that Catholics in Georgia in the late nineteenth century were gaining acceptance, anti-Catholicism began to spread. The American Protective Association, a Midwest organization that had arisen from fear of growing Catholic influence, was established in Georgia and soon ended the Catholic public school systems in Macon and Augusta. And the Ku Klux Klan renewed activities, which targeted Jews, African Americans, and Catholics.

Throughout the first half of the twentieth century, anti-Catholicism certainly continued to flourish in the American South, especially in provincial outposts. However, the growing ecumenical movement at midcentury signaled change, even in less-enlightened parts of the country. Furthermore, Pope John XIII and the reforms of the Second Vatican Council (1962–65) brought great change to the Roman Catholic Church, including such reforms as the use of the vernacular to replace the Latin Mass to better reflect the modern church's intentions for outreach, the changing of the position of the high altar so that the priest faces the congregation, and often subtle changes in the liturgy of the Mass itself to enable congregants to experience greater participation in the rite. Although Flannery O'Connor died before the closing of Vatican II, her letters indicate that she clearly approved of the "Aggiornamento," the fresh air invigorating the Church.

The crucified Christ,
Sacred Heart Catholic Church,
Milledgeville

The hand of the Virgin,
Sacred Heart Catholic Church

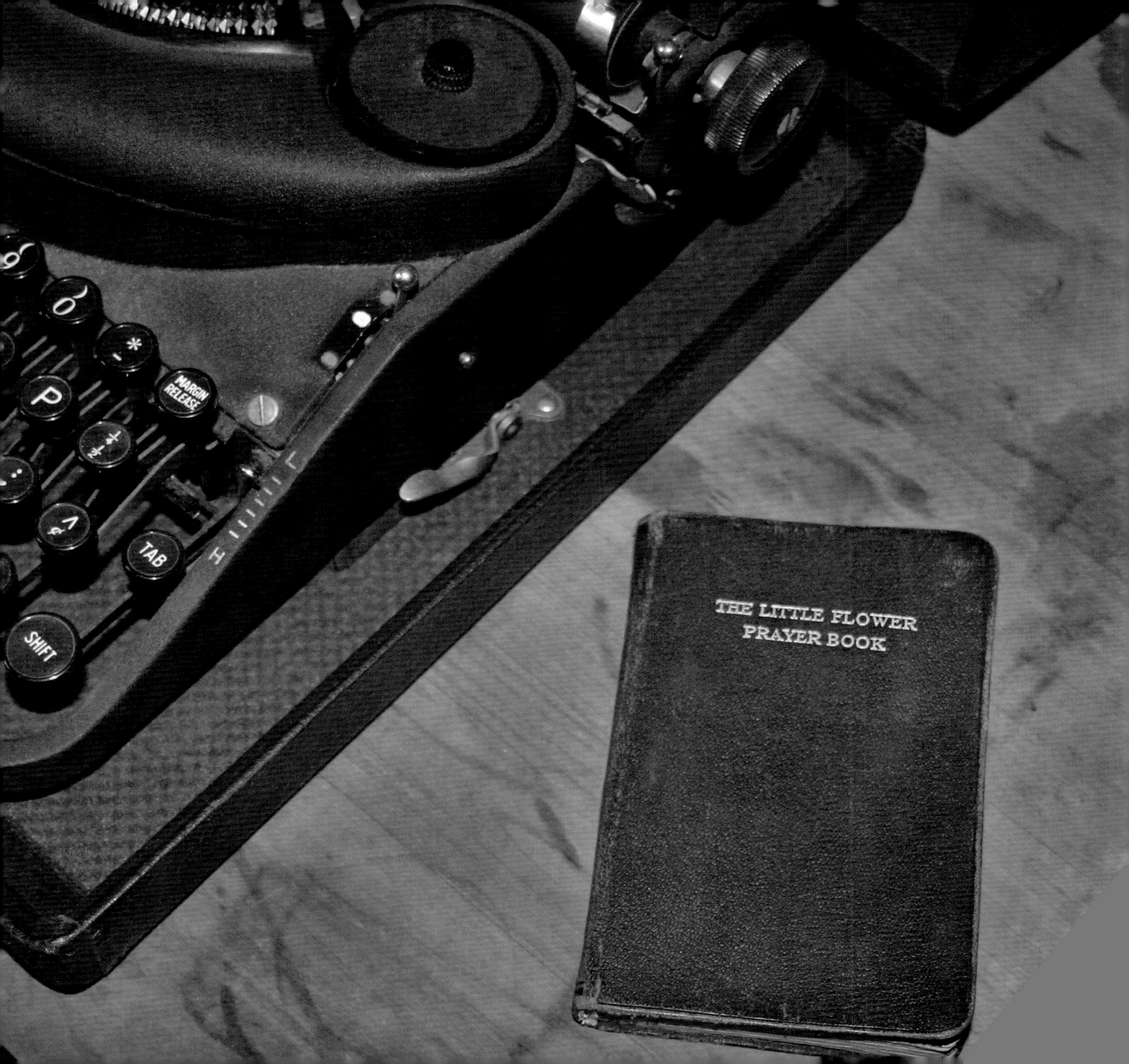

THE LITTLE FLOWER
PRAYER BOOK
MARGIN RELEASE
TAB
SHIFT

Catholicism in O'Connor's Fiction

THE ROMAN CATHOLIC CHURCH was at the center of Flannery O'Connor's life. A "cradle Catholic," O'Connor saw her Catholicism as liberating to her as a writer: "I feel that if I were not a Catholic, I would have no reason to write, no reason to see, no reason ever to feel horrified or even to enjoy anything. I am a born Catholic, went to Catholic schools in my early years, and have never left or wanted to leave the Church."

At the center of Catholicism is, of course, the Eucharist, or the celebration of the Mass, about which O'Connor made her oft-quoted statement to apostate Catholic Mary McCarthy, who argued in a sophisticated New York gathering that the Eucharist was a powerful symbol. O'Connor's retort, "If the Eucharist were only a symbol, I'd say to hell with it," is a stunning reminder of the strength of her belief.

The sacramental vision of life espoused by the Roman Catholic Church underlies all of O'Connor's fiction. Perhaps nowhere is that fact more evident than at the conclusion of "A Temple of the Holy Ghost." There, the sun, which gains in its association with the divine as the story proceeds, is described as "a huge red ball like an elevated Host drenched in blood," and as the sun sinks, it leaves "a line in the sky like a red clay road hanging over the trees." Christ's entry into human history and his sacrificial death for the sins of humankind are clearly suggested in these lines, as is Christ's presence among the least of us. The poetry of Jesuit priest Gerard Manley Hopkins, whom O'Connor greatly admired, is analogous to and influen-

Mary Flannery O'Connor at age three. Courtesy, Flannery O'Connor Collection, GCSU Library

OPPOSITE: *One of Flanner O'Connor's prayer books*

tial on O'Connor's sense of the God immanent in creation. O'Connor stories that perhaps most strongly suggest the presence of God are "The River," "The Displaced Person," "A View of the Woods," "Revelation," and "Parker's Back," all of which demonstrate—in brief lyrical passages rare in O'Connor's work—the mysterious efficacy of the divine in the world.

O'Connor suggests that only the spiritually myopic or the arrogantly self-sufficient are unable to perceive the Mystery. In "A View of the Woods," for example, the greedy and egotistical Mr. Fortune, aptly named, is finally unable to recognize the majesty and power of God and the gift of His Son to the fallen world:

> The third time he got up to look at the woods, it was almost six o'clock and the gaunt trunks appeared to be raised in a pool of red light that gushed from the almost hidden sun setting behind them. The old man stared for some time, as if for a prolonged instant he were caught up out of the rattle of everything that led to the future and were held there in the midst of an uncomfortable mystery that he had not apprehended before. He saw it, in his hallucination, as if someone were wounded behind the woods and the trees were bathed in blood.

O'Connor was acutely aware of the vulnerable position of Catholics throughout the state's early history, although in her mature work she chose to satirize the provincial stereotyping of Catholics in the South through such characters as Hoover Shoats, also known as Onnie Jay Holy, in *Wise Blood*; the Shortleys in "The Displaced Person"; and Asbury in "The Enduring Chill."

In *Wise Blood*, Hoover Shoats, mimicking Hazel Motes and his Church Without Christ, presents his church as one that can be relied on because "it's nothing foreign connected with it," "you don't have to believe nothing you don't understand and approve of," and "it's based on your own personal interpitation [sic] of the Bible." In fact, he says, "You can sit at home and interpit your own Bible however you feel in your heart it ought to be interpited . . . just the way Jesus would have done it." Here O'Connor wields a two-edged sword; she acknowledges the primitive misconceptions about Catholicism rampant in the South and underscores those practices of fundamentalist Protestantism with which she, as a Catholic, would have difficulty—for example, the lack of obedience to any teaching and moral authority outside the individual's own (often ignorant and self-serving) will, and, as corollary to that, the presumed freedom of the individual to read the Bible and find his or her own meaning there.

O'Connor presents that ignorance in Mr. and Mrs. Shortley of "The Displaced Person," both of whom view the priest who brings the Polish family to Mrs. McIntyre's farm as a sinister presence who has "come to destroy." Mr. Shortley is fearful that the "Pope of Rome" is going to begin dictating even the domestic habits of American daily life; his wife considers herself a visionary and believes the "end times" are being anticipated by the presence of the Catholic priest and the foreigners. For her part, Mrs. McIntyre, the Shortleys' employer, is also ignorant of the teachings of Christianity; she may be even more culpable than the Shortleys because she, a white woman of some means, has the necessary education and opportunity to be otherwise. Like the character of Hoover Shoats, the Shortleys are treated comically by O'Connor, whereas Mrs. McIntyre, the story's central character, receives more serious attention from the author, implying the adage that much is to be expected from those to whom much has been given. The priest in this early story is distracted and bumbling, but, unlike Mrs. Shortley, he is a true visionary who experiences and understands the Mystery of God as embodied in the peacock; he is the only character who does so. At the very least the priest, who is, incidentally, never named, is the visible reminder of the Mystery that Mrs. McIntyre has been unable to fathom, as he administers the last rites to Mr. Guizac. Mrs. McIntyre doesn't understand the sacrament and, even more significantly, has so devalued human life—seeing all of her farm workers as "extra"—

"'I ain't going to have no Pope of Rome tell me how to run no dairy,' Mr. Shortley said." ("The Displaced Person")

that she finally colludes in Mr. Guizac's murder. Here, however, the priest functions primarily as an indirect catalyst to Mrs. McIntyre's encounter with God. While he is surely the gentle antidote to Mr. Shortley's idea of the powerful, grasping Roman Catholic Church, his function is ancillary to the story's central action.

In O'Connor's posthumously published collection of stories, *Everything That Rises Must Converge* (1964), "The Enduring Chill" may signal at least a subtle recognition of changing attitudes toward Catholicism in the South. Here the priest is central to the story's denouement. Asbury Fox, the would-be writer who is the story's protagonist and who is, we assume, nominally a Protestant, believes that he has come home to die and orders his mother to summon a priest—most specifically, a Jesuit who will be his intellectual equal, or so he imagines. What the proud young man gets in the way of a priest, however, is exactly what he doesn't know he needs: a no-nonsense cleric, Father Finn from Purgatory (the name of his parish serving O'Connor's purpose very well), who immediately gets to the heart of Asbury's spiritual affliction by asking blunt questions about the young man's spiritual practices. He inquires of Asbury whether he has said his morning and evening prayers and admonishes him for not praying regularly: "You cannot love Jesus unless you speak to Him." When Asbury tries to demonstrate his sophistication by mythologizing the Deity, the old priest does not respond; instead he asks Asbury, "Do you have trouble with purity?" and continues by reviewing the catechism: "Who made you?" and "Why did God make you?" By this time Asbury knows he has made a mistake and tries to get rid of the priest by saying "I'm not a Roman." Not content to let Asbury off the hook, the priest responds by urging Asbury to ask for the Holy Spirit, though the arrogant "sick" boy replies, "The Holy Ghost is the last thing I'm looking for!" Angrily, the priest retorts, "How can the Holy Ghost fill your soul when it's full of trash? . . . The Holy Ghost will not come until you see yourself as you are—a lazy ignorant conceited youth!" And as Father Finn is leaving the house, Asbury hears him say to his mother, "He's a good lad at heart but very ignorant." This statement is undoubtedly the last straw for Asbury, who believes himself anything but ignorant!

Thus in one of her last stories, O'Connor allows the Catholic priest the pivotal role in effecting Asbury's revelation, and the descent of the Holy Ghost, figured in the watermark on his bedroom ceiling, *is* indeed the last thing that Asbury gets. Unlike the Shortleys, the presumably intellectual and sophisticated character is the epitome of the worst sort of ignorance, the spiritual kind. The Catholic priest, Father Finn, is neither the distracted, rather dotty cleric of "The Displaced Person" nor the handsome and saintly Bing Crosby of popular film in the 1940s. He is almost what one might call a Catholic fundamentalist, an unsentimental figure who, arguably, has a great deal in common with the most zealous of his Protestant counterparts. It is certainly possible to read this later story as indicative of O'Connor's increasing understanding of what is common to all Christian faith, in the 1960s spirit of ecumenism, and of her willingness to bring Catholicism to the forefront of her fiction. As though underscoring this point, O'Connor's last unfinished novel, *Why Do the Heathen Rage* (of which only fragments remain), presents for the first time in O'Connor's work a Catholic protagonist. The evolution of O'Connor's fiction may indeed parallel the increasing acceptance of Catholicism in Georgia and in the South, or at the least, O'Connor's own sense of that acceptance.

"When she was gone, he lay for some time staring at the water stains on the gray walls. Descending from the top molding, long icicle shapes had been etched by leaks and, directly over his bed on the ceiling, another leak had made a fierce bird with spread wings. It had an icicle crosswise in its beak and there were smaller icicles depending from its wings and tail. It had been there since his childhood and had always irritated him and sometimes had frightened him. He had often had the illusion that it was in motion and about to descend mysteriously and set the icicle on his head." ("The Enduring Chill")

SELECT BIBLIOGRAPHY AND FILMOGRAPHY

WORKS BY FLANNERY O'CONNOR

Wise Blood. New York: Harcourt, 1952.

A Good Man Is Hard to Find. New York: Harcourt, 1955.

The Violent Bear It Away. New York: Farrar, 1960.

Everything That Rises Must Converge. New York: Farrar, 1960.

Mystery and Manners. New York: Farrar, 1969.

The Complete Stories. New York: Farrar, 1971.

The Habit of Being: Letters of Flannery O'Connor. Edited by Sally Fitzgerald. New York: Farrar, 1979.

Flannery O'Connor: Collected Works. Edited by Sally Fitzgerald. New York: Library of America, 1988.

WORKS ABOUT FLANNERY O'CONNOR

Amason, Craig R. "From Agrarian Homestead to Literary Landscape: A Brief History of Flannery O'Connor's Andalusia." *Flannery O'Connor Review* 2 (2003–4): 4–14.

Bacon, Jon Lance. *Flannery O'Connor and Cold War Culture.* New York: Cambridge University Press, 1993.

Bonner, James. *Milledgeville: Georgia's Antebellum Capital.* Macon, GA: Mercer University Press, 1985.

Cash, Jean. *Flannery O'Connor: A Life.* Knoxville: University of Tennessee Press, 2002.

Ciuba, Gary. *Desire, Violence, and Divinity in Modern Southern Fiction: Katherine Anne Porter, Flannery O'Connor, Cormac McCarthy, Walker Percy*. Baton Rouge: Louisiana State University Press, 2007.

Elie, Paul. *The Life You Save May Be Your Own: An American Pilgrimage*. New York: Farrar, 2003.

Gentry, Marshall Bruce, Ed. *Flannery O'Connor Review* (formerly *The Flannery O'Connor Bulletin*). Milledgeville: Georgia College & State University, 1972–present.

Giannone, Richard. *Flannery O'Connor: Hermit Novelist*. Urbana: University of Illinois Press, 2000.

Gordon, Sarah. *Flannery O'Connor: The Obedient Imagination*. Athens: University of Georgia Press, 2000.

New Georgia Encyclopedia. http://www.georgiaencyclopedia.org (accessed 2007).

O'Gorman, Farrell. *Peculiar Crossroads: Flannery O'Connor, Walker Percy, and Catholic Vision in Postwar Southern Fiction*. Baton Rouge, Louisiana State University Press, 2004.

Srigley, Susan. *Flannery O'Connor's Sacramental Art*. Notre Dame, Ind.: University of Notre Dame Press, 2004.

Sykes, John. *Flannery O'Connor, Walker Percy, and the Aesthetic of Revelation*. Columbia: University of Missouri Press, 2007.

Wood, Ralph C. *Flannery O'Connor and the Christ-Haunted South*. Grand Rapids, MI: Eerdmans, 2004.

FILMS

A Circle in the Fire. Directed by Victor Nunez, 1974. Chicago: Perspective Films, 1976 (16mm).

The Displaced Person. Adapted by Horton Foote, directed by Glenn Jordan. American Short Story Film Series. Chicago: Perspective Films, 1977 (16mm).

Wise Blood. Adapted by Benedict and Michael Fitzgerald, directed by John Huston. Universal Studios, 1979.

INDEX